TALKS

ON WRITING

ENGLISH

MJP
PUBLISHERS

TALKS
ON WRITING
ENGLISH

Arlo Bates

Chennai   New Delhi   Tirunelveli

ISBN 978-93-87826-14-4   **MJP Publishers**

All rights reserved   No. 44, Nallathambi Street,
Printed and bound in India   Triplicane, Chennai 600 005

MJP 445   © Publishers, 2018

Publisher   C. Janarthanan

Project Editor   C. Ambica

PUBLISHER'S NOTE

The legacy of a country is in its varied cultural heritage, historical literature, developments in the field of economy and science. The top nations in the world are competing in the field of science, economy and literature. This vast legacy has to be conserved and documented so that it can be bestowed to the future generation. The knowledge of this legacy is slowly getting perished in the present generation due to lack of documentation.

Keeping this in mind, the concern with retrospective acquiring of rare books has been accented recently by the burgeoning reprint industry. MJP Publishers is gratified to retrieve the rare collections with a view to bring back those books that were landmarks in their time.

In this effort, a series of rare books would be republished under the banner, "MJP Publishers". The books in the reprint series have been carefully selected for their contemporary usefulness as well as their historical importance within the intellectual. We reconstruct the book with slight enhancements made for better presentation, without affecting the contents of the original edition.

Most of the works selected for republishing covers a huge range of subjects, from history to anthropology. We believe this reprint edition will be a service to the numerous researchers and practitioners active in this fascinating field. We allow readers to experience the wonder of peering into a scholarly work of the highest order and seminal significance.

MJP Publishers

PREFACE

These talks were given in the autumn of 1894 as a course on Advanced English Composition in the Lowell Free Classes, and that they are now printed is largely due to the fact that they were so well received by those who then heard them. In preparing them, I consulted whatever books upon composition came to my hand. I examined some with profit, some with pleasure, and some, it must be confessed, not wholly without amusement, or even impatience. Doubtless, I owe something to many of these books; but I am not conscious of much obligation to any save the "Principles of Rhetoric," by Professor A. S. Hill, "English Composition," by Professor Barrett Wendell, and "English Prose," by Professor John Earle.

I have conscientiously endeavored to make the lectures as practical as possible, stating as clearly as I could those things which would have been most helpful to me had I read and heeded them twenty years ago. The necessity of holding an audience made fitting some effort to render the talks entertaining; but I have never consciously said anything for the mere purpose of being amusing, and I have never been of the opinion that a book gains either in dignity or in usefulness by being dull. My purpose has throughout been sincerely serious, and if the book shall prove helpful, I shall have attained the object for which it was written.

A. B.

CONTENTS

I

The Art of Writing

Into all productive art enter two sorts of power, that which is communicable and that which is incommunicable,—in other words, that which may be taught and that which is inborn. Upon this fact is based the distinction between the mechanical and the fine arts, although since both kinds of power have a share in all production nobody has ever been able to draw a sharp and definite line at which the mechanical arts end and the fine arts begin. The power which is incommunicable is that of imagination, that indefinable grace and skill, that enchantment of creative ability which is born with rare individuals, and for which he who is not dowered with it by nature struggles in vain. It is this which has given rise to that saying as profound as it is terribly hackneyed which declares that a poet is born and not made. It is this which distinguishes genius from talent; and it is this which has so dazzled the eyes of the world as to produce the mistaken notion that since imagination is not to be learned nothing is to be learned in the realm of art.

This incommunicable power is the soul of fine art; yet into fine art no less than into the mechanical arts comes also that power which may be learned. This communicable power is commonly spoken of as the technical, or as technique. This any person of intelligence and perseverance can and may master if he choose, every man according to his ability; and this every artist must acquire, no matter how richly he may have been gifted by nature with the magic power which transcends and dominates it. It is this that musicians, painters, sculptors, architects, dancers, and writers are set to learn when they are said to study art. The world has long recognized that in painting, music, sculpture, and architecture it is indispensable that technique shall be acquired; but—absurd as it may seem—it is only recently, comparatively speaking, that it has been practically recognized that this is as true of poetry as of painting, as true of literature as of any other art. It is in truth only in our own day that there has been anything like a general acceptance of the fact that in literature as in the other arts technical skill must be laboriously acquired before any successful and permanent work can be produced. The masters have of course known this; but the idea that to be an author nothing is needed but pen, ink, and paper used to hold undisputed sway over the popular mind, and is by no means extinct yet. Not long ago I heard a learned professor in one of the leading American colleges declare that he could not see what there is to learn in composition. Last summer a gentleman of really wide reading, but who was brought up under the old system, said to me: "By teaching composition, I suppose you mean chiefly correcting the grammar and punctuation." He was somewhat surprised when I explained that students were supposed to have mastered both grammar and punctuation before the teaching of composition as such could begin.

The truth is that there has never been anything like a popular understanding of the difference between spoken and written speech. Anybody is supposed to be able to talk, and to learn to do so unconsciously,—a doctrine to which I do not wish to be understood as giving assent!—and it has been held to follow that anybody could write. To write was merely to talk with the pen, and that has commonly been held to be all there is to the matter save for the fact that some persons were born to write and some were not.

A personal experience of my own illustrates this, if its introduction may be pardoned. I have never forgotten the general bewilderment with which my friends met my announcement when I left college that I meant to study literature. That one should follow literature as a profession was not entirely unintelligible, if it did suggest a dire mental weakness on the part of the young man who was rash enough to take such a resolution; but how one studied literature as a profession was beyond ordinary understanding. "You mean that you are going to write books," some said tentatively. My reply that such a possibility was presupposed in the study of literature just as the pleading of cases might be presupposed in the study of law only increased the difficulty of the confusing puzzle. It was of course understood that there was in the law something to study; but what, in the name of common sense, was there to study in literature? Books one sat down and wrote, and that was the whole of it; and I soon found the idea gaining ground that I only put the matter in this way for the sake of producing an impression, or perhaps of covering a fixed and reprehensible intention of doing nothing.

I thought then that I had some idea of what the study of literature really meant, and I gave such explanations as I could; but, alas, the incessant work of years has chiefly served to show me how inadequate my idea was, and how much more there is to be learned than I then had any notion of! Some of the things which experience has taught me I think may be of value to you; and in these lectures I shall try to state them, although I realize but too well how far I am from being able to cover or exhaust the subject. I shall, of course, say some things which all of you know already, and many things which some of you know. I hope, however, to say also some things which you have not thought of, and by arrangement and system to give fresh value and force to old ideas. It is not impossible that experience has shown me things which will be practically helpful to others. Any man who has wrought long at a craft is likely to be able to give suggestions valuable to those who have not. The sluggard is by the Scriptures referred to the ant not on account of her intellectual superiority, but solely because of her great practical training.

All discussion must begin with definition, either expressed or understood. There is of course no doubt that each of us has an idea what composition is, yet to be sure that we are agreed, it is necessary to state the meaning in which we use the term. Let us say, then:—

Composition is the art by which ideas and mental impressions are conveyed in written language.

Nothing could sound more simple; few things are more difficult of achievement. It is not hard to convey ideas, but it is by no means easy to be sure that they will arrive at their destination in good order. Impressions and ideas are delicate things, and are most liable to be injured in the passage. There are writers whose methods suggest an attempt to get eggs to market by shooting them from a cannon,—the eggs may arrive, it is true, but in what condition? The means must be adapted to that with which one is dealing. It is folly to attempt to carry soap-bubbles in a mealsack or leaden bullets in a lace handkerchief. The student of the art of writing has to learn to suit his means to the end sought. He must train himself to judge what manner of expression, of style, or treatment, will best serve to transfer ideas from his own mind to that of the reader. He must study the effect of words and of combinations of words; the value of suggestion, and of all the emotional effects possible in written words. He must train himself to be able to use language as a skillful swordsman uses his rapier, adapting it to every emergency, master of it always; he must learn to be dexterous, adroit, and full of resources.

Exactly to impart an idea or an impression to another human being is manifestly impossible. The character of the mind of the receiver necessarily affects and modifies whatever comes to it. The thing which we say to our closest friend strikes him in a way somehow and somewhat different from that which we intend. A poem by John Boyle O'Reilly expresses this so fully that I take leave to quote it:—

AT BEST

The faithful helm commands the keel,

From port to port fair breezes blow;

But the ship must sail the convex sea,

Nor may she straighter go.

So, man to man; in fair accord,

On thought and will, the winds may wait;

> But the world will bend the passing word,
> Though its shortest course be straight.
>
> From soul to soul the shortest line
> At best will bended be;
> The ship that holds the straightest course
> Still sails the convex sea.

I do not quote this merely as a matter of sentiment, but because it phrases one of the most insistent and practical difficulties with which every writer must contend. The study of literary art, and indeed of all art, is in one sense an effort at approximation. Perfect expression can never be reached, and the thing after which a writer strives is to approach more and more closely toward that complete transmission of meaning which is forever unattainable while the barriers of human individuality stand between mind and mind.

We recognize this fact as soon as we reflect. Bob, thinking of Betty, remarks to Jack that he does admire a pretty girl; and Jack, fondly recalling the features of Jane, receives the idea with all the variations which belong to an altogether different idea of feminine loveliness. Tom, Dick, and Harry, returning from the races, declare to one another that it has been a jolly day. Each accepts the statements of his companions according to his individual experiences, and no one has imparted precisely the thought which was in his own mind. We praise a picture, a piece of music, a sunset, and the friend to whom we speak listens with a temperament and cultivation so different from our own that our words inevitably mean one thing to us and another to him. The ear which hears has always its share in the impression produced as surely as has the tongue that speaks.

The result might be much the same whether the words in these cases were spoken or written; but there is another element which makes an immense difference between oral and written communication. The speaker adds to his words a language of emphasis, of inflection, of facial expression, of gesture, of mien. He modifies what he says by what he looks; his bearing has as important a share in the work of conveying impressions as have his words. Two actors taking the same text will give characters so different as hardly to seem to have anything in common. A speaker may so contradict and override his speech that his hearer believes not the tongue that speaks, but the personality and manner which declare the contrary. You remember how Emerson puts this: "What you are stands over you the while, and thunders so that I cannot hear what you say to the contrary."

Now the writer is confronted by the necessity of making himself intelligible without the many aids by which the speaker may help out or modify his oral communication. The novelist, it is true, may avail himself of the simple device of describing the manner in which his characters speak. He tells us that this was said with a sly look of coquetry, while that was uttered in a voice of utter misery, and the other thundered forth in tones of overmastering determination. My washing came home in London last summer wrapped in a newspaper containing an installment of a blood-curdling tale which began thus: "Eleanore shot at Reginald from under her pellucid brows a lingering look of lurid hate." All this, however, is at its best ineffective and unsatisfactory, even when heroines have pellucid brows and the author is master of the art of alliteration. Some things are within the province of language and some are not.

Words may describe form, color, sound, and motion, but they can reproduce none of them. What they can do is to call up in the mind of the reader something which he has seen; or aid him to construct from material in his memory some new image. If one read a description of a landscape, for instance, he unconsciously selects bits of nature which he remembers and arranges them as nearly as may be after the pattern which the author gives. On the first page of "Westward Ho!" there is a description of—

> the little white town of Bideford, which slopes upward from its broad
> tide-river paved with yellow sands, and many-arched old bridge where
> salmon wait for autumn floods, toward the pleasant upland on the west.

Above the town hills close in, cushioned with deep oak woods, through which juts here and there a crag of fern-fringed slate; below they lower, and open more and more in softly-rounded knolls, and fertile squares of red and green, till they sink into the wide expanse of hazy flats, rich salt marshes and rolling sand-hills, where Torridge joins her sister Tor, and both together flow quietly toward the broad surges of the bar, and the everlasting thunder of the long Atlantic swell.

The reader constructs the picture as he goes on; but unless he has actually seen "the little white town of Bideford" the picture in his mind is likely to bear no very close resemblance to the reality. The broad tide-river which his fancy sees is some stream of his boyhood's home, and far enough from North Devon; the many-arched old bridge may be one which he knows or which comes to his memory from a picture,—perhaps from a photograph that a friend has brought from abroad of some hoary stone structure spanning a French river or a stream of Italy. The hills and the fern-clad cliffs are recalled in the same way, their outlines identical with the curves of some spot in the Catskills, in Wales, in Brittany, or wherever the reader is most familiar or has been most impressed. It is evident that the most carefully elaborate verbal description could not enable the artist to reproduce a scene; and herein is manifest the limitation of words in this direction.

The inadequacy of words becomes the more evident when it comes to matters intellectual. Who has not, even in conversation, experienced that baffled and hopeless feeling which comes from not being able to make another understand? Who does not know the sensation of being shut in as by walls of stone, so that it is impossible to reach the comprehension of the one addressed? Yet the speaker has a hundred advantages over the writer. He has at command all the resources of gesture, of look, accent, tone, mien. No man has written much and written earnestly without experiencing moments of complete despair in regard to being able to convey to his readers that which it is in his heart to say.

How far it is possible to overcome the obstacles which hinder communication is the study of the literary—as of every—artist. We human beings are prisoned in the solitary confinement of the body, and must needs devise means of sharing our thoughts, as political convicts in the Russian prisons strive to communicate by rapping on the walls. Every device by which intelligence may be carried more safely and surely is an addition to the intellectual resources and strength of the race. On this power of mutual transference and understanding of thought depends the whole intellectual progress of men, and on individual mastery of it rests the ability to share that progress.

It is only by the most careful and patient labor, the most rigid self-discipline, that advance can be made in a matter so difficult and so delicate. If you have supposed that the art of composition is one easily acquired, I beg you to lay aside that idea at the start. It is true that any person who has had an ordinary school training may write a poor letter or a badly bungled paragraph. Some even attain to a respectable facility in the superficial expression of ordinary ideas. To go beyond this, however, to arrive at being able really to write, to be capable of expressing with the pen genuine thoughts and real emotions with a reasonable hope that these will reach the reader not entirely distorted out of all resemblance to what they were when they left the mind of the writer,—this requires labor long and strenuous. The devils of incoherence, obscurity, and incompetency go not out save by untiring striving and watching.

This is strikingly illustrated by the great gulf between amateur and professional work. Many newspaper reporters are ignorant and intellectually untrained; yet merely from continuous and earnest practice they become so dexterous in the use of words as to be able to serve their needs with surprising facility. I have had well educated and cultivated men come into my office when I was an editor, and spend an hour in trying satisfactorily to phrase some simple announcement which they wished printed. All that there was to do was to say that such a charity needed funds, that a subscription had been opened, or some learned society was to meet at such a time and place; yet the amateur would struggle with the paragraph in an agony of ineptitude which was alike pathetic and farcical. When at last the conflict between mind and matter ended from the sheer exhaustion of the mind, there would be handed to me a scrawled sheet, recrossed and rewritten, and in the end a miracle of obscurity and awkwardness,—the art of how not to say it illustrated to perfection. Then after the visitor had taken himself off, in a condition not far from nervous exhaustion, it was only necessary to say to a reporter: "Make a paragraph of these facts." In a couple of minutes the slip would be ready to send to the printer, written in English not elegant, but easy and above all clear. The reporter had very likely not a hundredth part of the information or the experience of life of the amateur, but he had had continued business-like drill. He had written as a matter of steady work, with the improving consciousness of an editorial blue pencil ever before his mind. I have seen many definitions of the difference between amateur and professional work. To my own mind it has always seemed sufficient to say that the professional is one who has learned how to do a thing while the amateur is one who has not.

Closely connected with the difficulty of saying a thing is the difficulty of knowing when it is said. Anybody may write, but only the trained writer is able to be sure that what he has written says what he supposes it to say. This is of course doubly true from the need that there is of making words impart mood as well as meaning, the atmosphere as well as the facts. If it is hard to express ideas, it is doubly hard to embody also the state of mind from which they spring and which must be understood before their real value and significance can be appreciated. Not only is it far from easy to know when the written word will express what is meant; it is no less hard to be sure how much of a thought is actually on paper. It requires great effort to realize that the sentence or the paragraph which we write will not mean to the reader all that we wish him to understand. The thought in our mind is so vivid, so poignant, so vital, that for us the words brim over with significance as a full honeycomb drips with honey. The emotion which we feel in writing seems to belong inevitably to what is written, and to be inseparable from it. It is of all things most difficult for the author, especially in an impassioned mood, to put himself in the place of the cool and unmoved public; yet in no other way is it possible to judge how that public will be affected; in no other way is it possible to compare what is written with what is intended; to estimate the power of those poor black conventional signs there on the paper to express the thought and the mood, the glow and the fervor of head and of heart which it is their mission to carry vibrating and alive to the mind and the spirit of the reader.

It has often been remarked that authors are apt to be most fond of works which are not their best, and it is notorious that the most passionately poetic mood may be that in which a writer produces his least effective compositions. It is easy to see how this is connected with the point under consideration. In the aroused, imaginative, ecstatic mood every word is suggestive, every phrase full of meaning, each sentence rich with emotion. The writer who is carried away by his feelings is apt to go beyond the range of his judgment. He puts down the sign of his mood in language intelligible only to himself. He writes a sort of emotional shorthand, illegible to every eye except his own. To him it may remain beautiful because to him it recalls the exalted mood which produced it. To him it is the significant and sufficient memorandum of a thing beautiful and sublime; to others it is but a mass of words left by the elusive

Fancies which broke through language and escaped.

Dr. Holmes has said, with that quaint mingling of wit and wisdom which made him unique, that writing a poem is like pouring syrup out of a pitcher,—some of it always sticks to the pitcher. The principle holds good of all composition, and by no means the smallest thing to be learned is to judge how completely the syrup has been poured out. Often it is necessary to let the mood pass away entirely before one can estimate work. It is frequently well to let a manuscript lie by until the original enthusiasm of creation has faded fully, whether this process requires more or less time than the nine years which Horace recommended as the proper period during which a poem should remain unpublished.

It is perhaps not necessary to speak much of the value of a mastery of the art of composition; but there is one point which needs to be touched upon. There is a prevalent if not generally spoken idea that while this skill is an excellent thing, it is really necessary to nobody save professional writers; that while persons who give their lives to writing must of course master technique, it is not at all worth while for others to bother about a thing so difficult. That this error is less wide-spread than of old is evident from the increased attention which is everywhere given to composition in all modern schemes of education; but it survives in popular misapprehension. The truth is, on the contrary, that as society is organized to-day it is essential that every man or woman who hopes to make his or her way, at least to anything like eminence even comparative, shall be able to write fairly good English. In a world so largely dominated by the printing-press as is ours in these modern days, not only has the man who can express himself in ink a manifest advantage, but he who cannot is hampered from the start. The highest skill in composition which can be acquired is of instant practical value in every profession. Students of technical and scientific subjects seem to me to be as truly acquiring practical training when they are improving their skill in writing as when they are performing experiments in the laboratory or smelting ores at the furnaces. In reports to corporations, papers on sanitary engineering addressed to city officials, schemes for railroads or telegraphs laid before legislative committees, they will have need of all the literary cleverness that they can compass, all the literary skill which they are able to acquire. Competition is fierce all along the line, and facility in the use of the pen counts in every trade and in every profession no less truly than it does among avowed writers.

Nor is this the whole of the matter. Into every-day, common experience has the modern habit of life brought the need of being master of expression; and even he who does not put pen to paper—if it is possible to suppose such a person to exist among intelligent people—is under the necessity of cultivating his knowledge of the art of expression to the end that he may read more intelligently and more sensitively. There is great need of establishing communication with our fellow-men; there is hardly less need of learning to establish communication with ourselves. It seems sometimes as if our beings were like those Chinese carved balls which Tennyson calls

Laborious orient ivory sphere in sphere.

We strive to make our different selves know one another, but we find it hard. We are conscious of feelings, of ideas, of emotions, which some sphere of our manifold being knows, yet which to us—to the outer sphere, to the external Ego, so to say—are vague and distant however keenly we long to understand. The ability to phrase for others is soon found to be ability to phrase for ourselves. By no means the least of the advantages, as it is one of the greatest of the delights, of conquering expression, is the power of interpreting ourselves to ourselves.

There is a crude popular idea that the refinements of literary art are wasted, at any rate upon the general reader. So many books succeed, at least temporarily, which can make no slightest pretense to any grace of manner, and which have not even the merit of reasonable accuracy, that the student is apt to feel that these things are superfluous.

Of course the ordinary reader does not perceive delicate shades of expression, fine distinctions of phrase, or subtile beauties of style. Very likely he does not pause to consider whether a style is good or bad; and certainly he would be unable to analyze its merits if he attempted this. It does not follow that these graces do not touch him. It is by means of them that deep and lasting effects are produced. Susceptibility to artistic beauty is not necessarily conscious. Frankly, it is to be admitted that for the instant, evanescent, lurid success of sensational popularity it is not necessary to write good English. Books outside of the furthest stretch of charity in workmanship and style have, each in its day, the dazzling, however transient, success of a Roman candle or a rocket. In far too many newspapers one may see how flippant pertness and vulgar sharpness can dispense with the smallest shred of good style, may ignore syntax, scorn accuracy, and outrage decency itself.

Once for all it must be allowed that whoever seeks this sort of success need not waste his time in the study of English composition. The author of the latest scandalous novel never experiences the necessity of any exhaustive acquaintance with rhetoric, or even of knowing much more than the outside of the English grammar. The young women who are employed by enterprising journals to scramble around the world in the briefest possible time with a hand-satchel for luggage are apt to be as little encumbered with syntax as with trunks. The purveyors of gossip to society papers are not in the least obliged to know the language in which they attempt to convey their precious information. If they can discover that Mrs. Cholmondely-Jones is at the Sea View House, their readers are not troubled at the declaration that this leader of fashion is "stopping at the hotel for a week;"—confusingly impossible as such a feat may appear.

All this has been said over and over, and I repeat it here simply by way of reminder that there is no claim that popular success is not to be won without literary merit; any more than it could be claimed on the other hand that popular success is insured by it. It is certain that no permanent literary work can be accomplished without the mastery of a good English style; and it is equally certain that command of written language is of the highest value and use. Sensational books make their way not because of their crudities of style and their inaccuracies, but in spite of them. If to the qualities which have given them vogue had been added literary merit, they might have reached to permanent in place of temporary success. Certainly if a writer desires to impress, to persuade, to move, to arouse; if he have a report to write which he hopes may be adopted, a theory to state which he is in earnest to have received; a history to relate that he would have believed; an appeal that he longs to have heeded, a creation of the imagination by which he aims to touch the emotions of his fellow-men, he cannot too carefully cultivate the art of communicating it. In any of these cases mastery of literary technique is as essential to success as is air to breathing or light to seeing.

II

Methods of Study

The question remains: How is skill in composition to be gained? The general principle is as simple as the details of the craft are complicated. The way to write is to write. Perhaps the most exact image of the process is that of piano-playing. Just as one acquires skill in the use of the piano by innumerable exercises and continual practice, so one attains to mastery in written language only by writing and writing and writing. It is necessary to compose and recompose; to write all sorts of things, to prune them, recast them, polish them; to elaborate and to simplify; to weigh each word and phrase; and when all is done to destroy the result as ruthlessly as we would destroy anything else which has become rubbish by outliving its usefulness.

This last point needs to be insisted upon. Personal vanity and that interest in self which is so naturally and so universally human, work constantly to persuade the beginner that his poorest trials are worth preservation. In the case of the pianist, the sound of the five-finger exercise dies on the air, and there is luckily an end of it. The player cannot gather it up and send it to a magazine. He cannot even without great risk of encountering personal violence impose it upon the friend whom he has invited to dine. With the writer it is unhappily different. His first verses he sends cheerfully and a little condescendingly to a magazine. His second he distributes on privately printed slips to his friends,—and any acquaintance will serve as a friend in the distribution of privately printed poems! His third effort is apt to go to some overworked man of letters, accompanied by a note delicately hinting that the inclosure is better than anything which the recipient has done, and requesting him to have it published at once in one of the leading magazines.

It is a thousand pities that the work of writers who are learning their art is not written in ink fading over night, or which would at least vanish as soon as the manuscript had undergone revision. The next best thing is for the would-be author to accustom himself to phrasing thoughts in his mind without setting them down upon paper at all. This habit is of great value from the constant training that it gives, and it is of value also because it takes its place as the study of form for the sake of form; the effort to attain technical excellence unhampered by any consideration of producing compositions permanent in themselves.

The best technical training is that which is entirely disassociated from any idea that permanent work is being done. No one can get on very well or very far in English composition who is not able patiently and faithfully to do a great deal of work simply for the sake of learning how to do it, entirely realizing that the thing produced is of no value when it is done. It is as absurd to preserve or to attempt to publish these crude experiments as it would be to practice the five-finger exercises in public, and to attempt to persuade music-lovers to pay to come and hear them. Every editor knows what need there is of saying this. Each mail carries to the office of every magazine scores of manuscript which are nothing but the crude exercises produced in more or less unintelligent struggles with the art of composition. The soul of the editor faints within him, while on the other hand the misguided, sensitive, self-conscious writer is smitten to the heart when his or her exercise is sent back with a printed card declining it with a hollow mockery of thanks. It is ludicrously pathetic; and I dwell upon it a little because in my time I have been foolish enough to offend in this manner; because as an editor I suffered enough from this cause to square the account beyond the cavil of the most exacting fate; and because in the course of my literary life I have seen so much of this sort of thing that I realize how general the experience is. It would be of less moment were it not for the depth of despair into which would-be authors are plunged by the return of these exercises. There is no despair like the despair of youth, and it makes my heart tingle now to recall the utter anguish with which I have received rejected early manuscripts—which should never have been sent to a publisher. Would to heaven that there were some one eloquent enough to persuade the world once and for all that literature is as surely a profession which must be learned as is law or medicine. No delicate woman or sensitive man, thrown suddenly upon her or his own resources, turns to law or medicine, expecting to gain a livelihood by practicing these professions uninstructed; yet this would be hardly less logical than to expect to make a way in literature without long preparation and study. Nobody seems to believe this. It is probably disbelieved now, as I say it; and examples of persons who have succeeded in writing with no apparent training come to mind at once. It would be idle to retort to objections of this sort that quacks have succeeded in all professions; and I must content myself with insisting that whether what I have been saying is believed or not, it is true, and the proofs are heart-sickeningly familiar to every man of literary experience at all extended.

It is important to remember that the best technical training is that in which nothing is considered but technical excellence. The student should write with his entire attention fixed upon the technical excellence of the work. He must think not of what he is doing, but of how he is doing it. It is a long time before the student has a right to look upon himself as a producer at all; and the more completely he can preserve the attitude of a learner, the better will be the results of his self-training.

Guy de Maupassant, one of the most finished masters of literary art, pure and simple, who have written in this century,—a writer who achieved so much, and who lacked only a supreme ethical ideal to do so much more,—indicates something of what is meant by technical training in composition in his account of his studies under Flaubert:—

Flaubert, whom I saw sometimes, conceived a friendship for me. I ventured to submit to him some of my attempts. He kindly read them, and said to me: "I cannot tell whether you have talent. What you have shown me proves a certain intelligence; but you must not forget this, young man,—that talent, in the phrase of Buffon, is only long patience. Work." ... For seven years I made verses, I made tales, I made novels, I even made a detestable play. Of them all nothing remains. The master ... criticised them, and enforced upon me, little by little, two or three principles, which were the pith of his long and perfect teaching. "If one has not originality," he said, "it is necessary to acquire it." Talent is long patience. It is a question of regarding whatever one desires to express long enough and with attention close enough to discover a side which no one has seen and which has been expressed by nobody. In everything there is something of the unexplored, because we are accustomed to use our eyes only with the thought of what has been already said concerning the thing we see. The smallest thing has in it a grain of the unknown. Discover it. In order to describe a fire that flames or a tree in the plain, we must remain face to face with that fire or that tree until for us they no longer resemble any other tree or any other fire. This is the way to become original.

Having, moreover, impressed upon me the fact that there are not in the whole world two grains of sand, two insects, two hands or two noses absolutely alike, he forced me to describe a being or an object in such a manner as to individualize it clearly, to distinguish it from all other objects of the same kind. "When you pass," he said to me, "a grocer seated in his doorway, a concierge smoking his pipe, a row of cabs, show me this grocer and this concierge, their attitude, all their physical appearance; suggest by the skill of your image all their moral nature, so that I shall not confound them with any other grocer or any other concierge; make me see, by a single word, wherein a cab-horse differs from the fifty others that follow or precede him." ... Whatever may be the thing which one wishes to say, there is but one word for expressing it; only one verb to animate it, but one adjective to qualify it. It is essential to search for this verb, for this adjective, until they are discovered, and never to be satisfied with anything else.—*Pierre et Jean*, Introduction.

I have given this long quotation because it puts the case so strongly, because it has the weight of authority so high in technical matters, and because it touches upon several points which will come up later. There are dangers in this method of which we shall speak in the proper place, but here the thing to be emphasized is the absolute indispensability of rigorous training when one is struggling to acquire the art of verbal expression.

Robert Louis Stevenson, that beautiful master of words, has also told us how he trained himself to that dexterity and grace which have been the delight of so great a company of readers:—

All through my boyhood and youth, I was known and pointed out for a pattern of an idler; and yet I was always busy on my own private end, which was to learn to write. I kept always two books in my pocket, one to read, one to write in. As I walked, my mind was busy fitting what I saw with appropriate words; when I sat by the roadside, I would either read, or a pencil and a penny version-book would be in my hand to note down the features of the scene or commemorate some halting stanzas. Thus I lived with words. And what I wrote thus was for no ulterior use. It was written consciously for practice.—*A College Magazine.*

It is well in learning to write to select uninteresting subjects; themes which depend for their effectiveness not upon what they are but upon the way in which they are presented. It is the natural tendency of any inexperienced writer to set to work to find something to write about which is in itself attractive. In the daily themes which I receive from students I find that the almost inevitable course of things is that the student writes upon whatever romantic or striking incidents have occurred in his life, and that when these are exhausted he is utterly at a loss for something to write about. It is not easy to persuade students that they will get training far more valuable out of careful attempts to express the commonplace. It is hard for eager young writers to follow the advice which Flaubert gave to De Maupassant. They are not willing to put their most strenuous efforts into the attempt to present vividly the grocer or the cab-horse. Yet there is nothing more valuable in training than to be thrown entirely upon one's own literary skill, be it much or little. When one deals with a subject fascinating in itself it is difficult to determine how much of the force of what is written depends upon the theme and how much may fairly be attributed to the treatment. In training which is purely technical it is essential to make this distinction, and it follows that the learner is wise to choose for his 'prentice efforts matters little attractive in themselves.

I have said that the way to learn to write is to write. It would perhaps be better to say that the way to learn to write is to rewrite. In the careful revision, the patient reconstruction, the unsparing self-criticism of the student who is determined to be satisfied with nothing short of the best of which he is capable, lies the secret of success. Here, as in everything else connected with the study of technique, patient, painstaking, untiring work is the essential thing.

In regard to revision it is necessary to call attention to the fact that it must extend to the revision of paragraphs and whole compositions. We are apt to confine ourselves to the remodeling and the polishing of sentences, or, if we get so far as to revise paragraphs, to take each separately. It is essential that we train ourselves to consider sentences as part of paragraphs and paragraphs as but portions of a whole. This it is especially hard for untrained writers to do. Those who have taught will recognize how difficult it is to make students realize that the sentences of a theme may all be individually right while yet the theme as a whole is all wrong.

As a matter of practical work it is well to make a schedule of chapters by paragraphs and of the whole composition by chapters, if the work be on so extensive a scale. It is one of the tests of a properly constructed paragraph that it can be roughly summed up in a single sentence, and a longer division may consequently be reduced in substance to as many sentences as there are paragraphs. It is an excellent plan thus to summarize work, and a little practice enables a writer to do this in his head without the trouble of putting the abstract upon paper.

It is evident that to learn the art of composition is no small undertaking, but it is to be kept in mind that this art, being the means of human expression, underlies all study and all thought no less than it underlies all communication. It aids one to understand what one reads, what one studies, what one thinks, no less than it aids one to compose a poem, to produce a novel, to write a letter, or to relate the latest bit of piquant gossip. Do not make the mistake of supposing that it is outside of your other intellectual pursuits, save in the sense that all the rest of your education is inclosed in it. We fully understand only that which we are ourselves capable of; and to comprehend the literature of the world it is necessary to come as near to being able to have produced it as is possible to our individual capabilities.

III

Principles of Structure

Since it is the object of this book first of all to be practical, it is well, before passing to matters more intricate, to consider for a little the elementary principles of composition.[1] Written language, to repeat what everybody knows, consists of words arranged in sentences, which in turn are grouped into paragraphs, these again being placed together to form whole compositions. In all composition, it may be remarked, it is necessary to remember that the punctuation is as integral and as important a part of what is written as are the words. It is often more easy to forgive the careless printer for altering a word than for changing punctuation, since the reader more easily corrects an error of diction than of pointing. The student has not mastered even the preliminary stages of composition who is not as sure of the punctuation of a page as he is of its grammatical construction.

There is a general vagueness on the subject of the mechanical forms employed in written or printed language which affects the nerves as if it were connected with the moral laxity of the age. There is probably no real connection between the frequency of bank defalcations and a failure to recognize the relative values of the comma and the semicolon, but to a literary man this ignorance is so culpable as almost to seem likely to lead to crime. When an inexperienced writer gets the words down he is apt to suppose that all is well, and frequently he does not even know when to put in a period. It is necessary not only to close a sentence when it is done, but also to bear in mind that if it

---

1   In this chapter and the next three I am so greatly indebted to Professor Barrett Wendell's "English Composition" that this part of my book might almost be called a summary of his, although I have of course omitted much and have introduced some things upon which he has barely touched

is not finished putting a period in the middle does not really make two sentences of it. When a tyro finds that his pen is getting out of breath, he has a tendency to set down a period, and then to go on with a conjunction, supposing, in the innocency of his heart, that he is beginning afresh. He is really only setting up the divorced better half—for the latter portion of a sentence should be the better half—in a sort of separate maintenance. The period in such a case has not even the power of a divorce, since it cannot make the separation legal. A sentence is like an ingot: if it be chopped in two, each piece is half of the original whole. It must be melted and recast to make individual ingots of smaller size.

It is also to be noted that students too often fail to recognize the fact that there are reasons as definite and as binding for the divisions of sentences into paragraphs as for the division of words into sentences. A teacher recently told me of the definition of a country schoolboy which, if not over-elegant, represents pretty fairly, it seems to me, the attitude of the common mind toward the paragraph. "A paragraph," this lad said blunderingly, when called upon to define, "why, a paragraph—a paragraph—it's—it's a gob of sentences!" I fancy that most teachers have encountered plenty of pupils who think of a paragraph as merely a "gob" of sentences,—a lump accidentally broken off from the rest of the composition, but possessed of no structural qualities of its own.

The analysis of sentences is common in schools, but, so far as I know, there is little analysis of paragraphs. To my thinking there is more to be gained from the latter than from the former. The analysis of the paragraph calls for a wider view, for a better comprehension of subject, and for a more developed idea of form. I do not wish to be understood as endeavoring to invent a new torture for pupils or one more device for further overburdening teachers already overloaded. I merely call attention to the value as a means of mental and literary training of the study of paragraph structure in the works of the masters of style, and to the fact that such study is an indispensable part of a literary training.

Of course the ultimate appeal in all that concerns the mechanics of composition is to what is commonly called Good Use. All written symbols by which intelligence is conveyed from man to man are arbitrary. It is merely because it is agreed that the character "I" shall represent a sound and that this sound shall stand for an idea, that we are able to bring up the idea in the mind of others simply by writing the sign. That there is nothing innate in the symbol is evident from the fact that other signs have been used to represent this sound, and that other syllables have stood for the pronoun in the first person singular. The examples which might be given to illustrate this point are limited only by the number of words in existence. Consciously or by tacit consent—oftener, of course, by the latter—it has been agreed to attach sounds to ideas and to represent those sounds by definite symbols. It follows that he who wishes to communicate an idea in writing has no resource outside of the means which have been agreed upon by the consent of his fellow-men. A writer may decide to have a new vocabulary and to write it in novel characters. The difficulty is that it will be understood by nobody. He is forced to use the language of men, and to use it in the fashion in which it is employed by others. He is bound by the habit of men who write, established by custom and defined by common acceptance. In other words, he is constrained to follow Good Use.

Good Use is the general agreement in regard to conventions by means of which ideas are conveyed. It is the basis of all composition, and without an intimate knowledge of it no one can write successfully. What the best general agreement is, is to be determined by the practice of the most eminent and widely recognized authors. The fact of their general indorsement and recognition is a sufficient proof that their use is intelligible to their public, and that it is therefore safe to follow them. Their custom decides not because of their authority, but because their reputation proves that their use is the one which is tacitly accepted by intelligent readers, and which is therefore the only one that will insure comprehension.

There are certain things which in writing it is necessary to keep constantly in mind until they are observed unconsciously and instinctively.

Always a writer must hold to three Principles of Structure and three Principles of Quality. The division is of course arbitrary, but it is logical and convenient. The three Principles of Structure,—the mechanical principles, so to say, those which direct most obviously the mechanics of language,—are Unity, Mass, and Coherence. The three Principles of Quality—those which govern the inner and more intellectual character of a composition—are Clearness, Force, and Elegance.

The first principle of structure, Unity, has to do with the substance of a sentence or a composition. It is the law which requires that every composition shall be informed with a general intention, shall centre around one fundamental idea; that every paragraph and every sentence shall be dominated by one essential thought or purpose. It is the principle which produces the difference between a well-ordered whole and an unorganized collection of scraps; between a rich embroidery and a sampler, a mosaic and a crazy-quilt. Without Unity as a whole a composition becomes as disjointed as a dictionary, without attaining to the instructiveness of that necessary book; and in degree only less from the proportionate importance of a part to the whole, the lack of Unity in a sentence destroys the value and effectiveness of the entire work.

The second principle, that of Mass, concerns the external arrangement of what is written. It is the rule which enjoins the putting of the chief parts of the composition, of the paragraph and of the sentence, in the places which most readily catch the eye or the ear. This is sometimes spoken of as Emphasis, but the term is hardly comprehensive enough. All questions of proportion come of course under the head of Mass, and so does whatever in the outward form of a composition appeals to the eye.

Coherence, the third principle of structure, is the law of internal arrangement. The relation of each part to the others must be made clear and unmistakable. We are all but too familiar with the style of writing which resembles the valley of dry bones of the prophet's vision, composition wherein the relation of one fragment to another is to be discerned only by the most careful research. Coherence is as the inspired prophecy of Ezekiel, whereby the bones came together, bone to bone, so that the valley was filled with an exceeding great army.

Unity is at once the simplest and the most easily secured of these three requirements. It is within the power of any writer of reasonable judgment to tell when the matter contained in a sentence concerns a single idea or several ideas so closely connected that they must belong together. It is a matter of perception, and for avoiding incongruous constructions there is perhaps no other rule so good as the simple injunction: Be sure that sentences have Unity. Every text-book upon rhetoric warns against this fault and contains examples of it. The writer who accustoms himself to realize vividly what he is saying is not likely to fall into the error.

The danger attending upon the effort to secure Unity is that of Dryness. The writer who is excessively careful about confining every sentence to a single thought and every paragraph to a single group of thoughts dominated by a central idea is sometimes likely to fail of variety and richness of structure. He becomes timid about admitting even proper ornaments, and gives to his style an air of being constructed upon the model of a wall of brick masonry. Variety is as essential to composition as is Unity, and it is necessary to be careful lest in securing one the other be lost. Every student should become sufficiently self-critical to know in which direction he is more likely to err, and to direct his efforts for improvement accordingly.

The question of Mass is more difficult. This principle governs the places of words and clauses in the sentence, of sentences in paragraphs, of paragraphs in longer compositions. The whole matter is admirably and succinctly put by Mr. Wendell:—

In any composition the points which most readily catch the eye are evidently the beginning and the end. From which, of course, it follows that, broadly speaking, every composition—sentence, paragraph, chapter, book—may conveniently begin and end with the words which stand for ideas that we wish to impress on our readers.... Broadly speaking, the office of punctuation is to emphasize,—to do for the eye what vocal pauses and stress do for the ear,—to show what parts of a composition belong together, and among these parts to indicate the most significant. It is clear that periods emphasize more strongly than semi-colons; and semi-colons than commas. From this, of course, it follows that in an ideally massed sentence the most significant words come close to the periods, the less significant close to the lesser marks of punctuation, the least significant in those unbroken stretches of discourse where there is nothing but words to arrest the eye. The test of a well-massed sentence, then, is very simple: Are the words that arrest the eye the words on which the writer would arrest your attention?

The application of this principle to books is easily seen, and perhaps is especially obvious in fiction. In an effective novel it will generally be found that some interesting and striking situation has been chosen for the beginning. Frequently the author makes a bold plunge into the very heart of the story in order to find an impressive passage with which to begin. The more important emphasis, that of the conclusion, must be properly employed or the entire effect of the work as a whole is sacrificed.

A good example of the ill effect of failing to employ the emphatic points of a book properly is afforded by Stanley J. Weyman's pleasing story, "My Lady Rotha." The first seven chapters are occupied with an account of the rebellion of a village against its chatelaine and of her flight from her castle to avoid their rage. Once the Lady Rotha is free of the castle, however, the book is devoted to her adventures in a country where the King of Sweden, the great Wallenstein, and numerous other leaders are filling the land with war and danger and bloodshed. To the very end of the tale the reader expects that the narrative will return to the castle, and that there will appear some better excuse for the opening chapters than the need of starting the heroine on her perilous travels; but the novel finishes without going back to the castle or telling how matters were settled there. The book is so badly massed that the very force of its beginning injures instead of aiding the effect of the whole.

In another and better tale by the same author, "A Gentleman of France," the first emphasis is given to the poverty and undeserved ill fortune of the hero; so that when in time fate leads him to better things the later joy is heightened by contrast with the earlier gloom. I take these two books because they have been widely read of late, but any novel that comes to hand is an illustration of one sort or another.

The danger to be avoided in endeavoring to secure effective massing of compositions is that of artificiality. This is especially obvious in the construction of sentences. In an uninflected language, like English, wherein the relative places of words are necessarily fixed more or less absolutely, it is not easy to re-order the arrangement without giving to the style an appearance of artifice. Dexterously to overcome this difficulty is one of the things which the student has to learn, and perhaps more upon the success with which he is able to do so than upon any other single thing will depend the effectiveness of what he writes.

The third principle of structure, Coherence, is one of which the lack is easily perceptible, but the securing of which is often difficult. The rule is that words closely related by their share in the thought to be conveyed shall be kept together,—and so stated is simple enough. No one, however, is likely to have written even a page upon any subject at all intricate without having to pause to rearrange the clauses of some involved sentence or of some confused paragraph. A great hindrance in the struggle for Coherence, it should be added, is a want of clear perception of what one wishes to say. The position of words is often determined by the choice of shades of expression which are extremely delicate, and unless the writer has an accurate and acute perception of these he cannot be sure of the order of his words and clauses.

It is easy enough to see how the phrases are misplaced in the stock examples of incoherence which are given in the books of rhetoric. Any novice could improve a sentence of this sort:—

He left off his old coat to marry a lady with a large Roman nose which had been worn continuously for ten years.

It takes only a little thought to see the error in the phrase:—

The crowd turns, departs, disintegrates;

where it is evident that the connection is between "turns" and "disintegrates," and that the crowd departs after it has broken up. Not less obvious, when attention is called to it, is the fault here:—

Lothair was unaffectedly gratified at *not only* receiving his friends at his own castle, *but* under these circumstances of intimacy.[2]

It is not hard to see the difference of meaning between these two sentences:—

So long as men had slender means, whether of keeping out cold or checkmating it with artificial heat, Winter was an unwelcome guest, especially in the country.

So long as men had slender means, especially in the country, of keeping out cold or checkmating it with artificial heat, Winter was an unwelcome guest.

It requires a more trained perception to feel the variations which result from altering in the following example the position of "only."

The theory that the poet is a being above the world and apart from it is true of him as an observer only who applies to the phenomena about him the test of a finer and more spiritual sense.—Lowell: *Life and Letters of James Gates Percival*.

If we say "is true only of him who as an observer," we shall mean one thing,—and I confess to a suspicion that this is the thing which Lowell intended!—whereas the passage as it stands asserts that the theory is true considering the poet as merely an observer.

It is not necessary to multiply examples. Every student who attempts careful expression will come upon illustrations enough in his own work. The important thing is to be clearly aware of what is to be said, and then to be sure that it is said, and said unmistakably.

---

2   Disraeli: Lothair. Quoted by Professor Hill.

In the construction of sentences the coherent arrangement of words is frequently hindered by the grammatical relations; no such limitation prevents the proper placing of sentences in the formation of paragraphs. In the construction of paragraphs, however, even more than in the construction of sentences, is necessary the utmost clearness of ideas. It is here essential to know not only what one has to say, but the relative strength which should be given to each link in the chain of thought. The question of proportion must here have the fullest answer. The relative stress which is to be given by position and the relative stress which is to be imparted by proportion are alike of the greatest importance in the making of the paragraph.

Something of this may be shown by an example. The following is a paragraph from the essay by Jeffrey on "The Characters in Shakespeare's Plays:"—

> Everything in him [Shakespeare] is in unmeasured abundance and unequaled perfection,—but everything so balanced and kept in subordination, as not to jostle or disturb or take the place of another. The most exquisite poetical conceptions, images, and descriptions, are given with such brevity, and introduced with such skill as merely to adorn without loading the sense they accompany.... All his excellences, like those of nature herself, are thrown out together; and instead of interfering with, support and recommend each other.

Let this now be read with a transposition of sentences:—

Although in Shakespeare everything is so balanced and kept in subordination as not to jostle or disturb or take the place of another, and is in unequaled perfection, yet everything is in an unmeasured abundance. He gives with such brevity and introduces with such skill as to adorn without loading the sense they accompany, the most exquisite poetical conceptions, images, and descriptions. All his excellences, although they support and recommend instead of interfering with each other, are thrown out together like those of nature herself.

The words and phrases are identical in these two paragraphs, save for the slight alterations and changes of connectives made necessary by transposition; and yet the effect is distinctly different. The first, as Jeffrey intended, remarks that in spite of the great luxuriance of Shakespeare's work it is always well ordered; the second declares that although well ordered the poet's work is as luxurious as nature herself.

If the proportion were changed, the effect would be varied again. Cutting out a few clauses from the original, we have:—

> Everything in Shakespeare is so balanced and kept in subordination as not to jostle or disturb or take the place of another. The most poetical conceptions are given with such brevity and introduced with such skill as merely to adorn without loading the sense they accompany. All his excellences are thrown out together, and instead of interfering with, support and recommend each other.

Here Shakespeare's fine ordering of his style is made more emphatic than in the original, and a glance will show how, by the suppression of other phrases, the luxuriance of his work could have been given the more prominence. A writer must know which of many possible shades of meaning is the one which he desires to convey, and he is likely to be successful in his work or the reverse according to the sharpness of his own apprehension of what he is aiming at. The gunner who shuts his eyes when he fires is more likel y to hit the mark than is the writer who vaguely endeavors to say something likely to succeed in accurately saying anything.

IV

Details of Diction

The student who endeavors to apply to words the tests of Good Use finds himself confronted with some questions which are very easily answered and with others so difficult that even the experts of language may disagree concerning them. It is of course to be supposed that we have all mastered the canons which forbid the use of Barbarisms, Improprieties, and Solecisms,—however much we allow ourselves to be influenced by the newspapers into the habit of violating them. We have not got through our early school years without having our attention called to the difference of effect produced by long and short words. Most of us have had more or less confusing instruction on the subject of the use of Latin words and words which are somewhat inexactly termed Anglo-Saxon. We have all known brief but bewildered intervals during which we endeavored to live up to a noble resolution to make our vocabulary strongly Anglo-Saxon; and we are most of us conscious in our secret hearts that we neither did this ever, nor ever for a moment knew how to set to work to do it.

It is as well for the written language of to-day that there has never been possible a practical revision of the tongue by the dropping of words of Latin origin. It is a most mistaken notion which turns attention to the race origin of words instead of directing study to their actual force in use. It sounds admirably learned to talk of a diction which is too strongly Latin or which is markedly Anglo-Saxon; it is possible enough to see that in general a preponderance of classical words imparts dignity and that an abundance of Saxon gives terseness to a style; but the man who in desiring to secure the one effect or the other goes to work to select his language on this basis is utterly ignoring the very first principles of practical composition. Words are to be chosen with reference to a desired effect, and their pedigree is of no more consequence than is that of the players on a foot-ball team. The boys of one descent may do better than those of another, and words of one or of another derivation may produce a desired effect,— but the contrary may be true, so that such a principle of selection is as absurd in one case as in the other.

Of long and short words much the same might be said. We are pretty well out of the days when it was still needful to insist upon the admonition of Frere:—

> And don't confound the language of the nation
>
> With long-tailed words in *osity* and *ation*.

The childish love of fine words which belongs to the infancy of literature is generally outgrown. It is recognized that words are to be selected solely for their effect, and not for extraneous pretensions. In this way is to be made the choice between words general and specific, and of words literal or figurative.

A consideration which is of importance in the choice of words, and one with which we shall be concerned later on, is that of denotation and connotation. A word denotes what it expresses directly; it connotes what it expresses indirectly; it denotes the idea which it names, and connotes the idea that it implies; it denotes what it says, and connotes what it suggests. The word "Washington" denotes a particular man, whose history we know, but with that history go so many suggestions and associations that the name connotes the idea of patriotism, military skill, and devotion to the nation from the very hour of its birth. The word "treason" denotes a specific offense against the government; while it connotes all the shame with which men regard one who betrays his country. In the familiar line of Wordsworth,

> A violet by a mossy stone,

the words denote a certain common flower beside a stone covered with another common and ordinary vegetable growth; they connote all the beauty of the azure blossom, the sweetness of the springtide, the quietude of a sylvan scene, all those lovely and touching associations which can be expressed only by suggestion. It is in the fact that certain sentiments can be conveyed by indirect means only that the value of connotation lies. To suggest by the choice of words those delicate and subtle ideas which are like a fragrance or like the iridescent sheen of nacre is one of the highest triumphs of literary art; and the nice artist in words is certainly not less careful in regard to the connotation of words than he is of their denotation.

One of the things which often puzzles beginners is how to increase their vocabulary. Of course reading is one of the most effective means of enlarging one's knowledge of the language,—but it is only careful reading, reading in which are studied the force and the color of terms as well as their literal meaning, that is of any marked value in this direction. It is said that Thackeray was in the habit of studying the dictionary with a frank purpose of adding to his knowledge of words. I have known two literary men who followed this practice, but they both deliberately selected unusual and bizarre examples with the avowed object of adding a unique and whimsical flavor to their journalistic work. Such an example is of course to be shunned, but in general there is far too little stress laid upon the use of the dictionary. There should be in every preparatory school a regular exercise in the use of the dictionary, and in it all students should be required to join. The teacher should read an extract or a sentence, or should give out words to the class, and have the meanings and derivations actually looked up at the moment. The differing values of synonyms should be examined; and if possible something of the history of the words given. The aim should be to encourage the student in the habit of having a lexicon at hand and of using it constantly.

Another important means of increasing one's command of language is conversation, and the value of conversation in this respect as in every other is in direct ratio to its character. To talk is not enough; it is necessary that the talker exert himself to do his best. Chatter is of no value as intellectual training; it is the exercise of the mind which tells. The subject of conversation may be as light as possible; but it is important that whatever is said is said well, whether it be a compliment to a mistress' eyebrow, a discussion of the deepest philosophy of life, or the latest bon-mot of the clubs. "Every variety of gift," Emerson says truly,—"science, religion, politics, letters, art, prudence, war, or love,—has its vent and exchange in conversation," and it follows that conversation properly conducted helps to the power of expression in all of these.

Better than all other means of increasing the vocabulary, however, is writing. Always the way to learn to write is to write. The way to increase one's power of expression is to strive to express. The habit of seeking constantly for the right word results in ability to find the right word. It acts not only directly, widening one's domain in the realm of language, but it renders a hundred-fold more effective the use of reading and of talk. It puts the mind into an attentive mood so that when a new term is met with it is remembered. The perception on the alert for words becomes susceptible to them, so that they are appreciated and retained. Cultivate the habit of putting things into words and the words will come unconsciously; practice phrasing thought and the means of phrasing it will not long be wanting.

When we go on from the consideration of words to that of sentences we find that here Good Use is more clearly defined. The rules for the construction of sentences are to a large extent more formal than those which govern the choice of terms, and the most obvious of them are conveniently collected and arranged under the name of Grammar.

Grammar is the account-book of custom; it is in reality a reckoning up of the popular suffrages in regard to verbal proprieties. In other words, grammar is the formal statement of the decisions of Good Use in so far as they apply to the relative forms of words. It is of course not necessary to speak here in detail of these. I only wish to call attention to the rules of the grammarian as a particularly well defined example of the supremacy of Good Use in all matters relating to language and its employment in literature. It is because the general consent has decided that a certain form of the verb shall be plural that the grammarian declares it to be in that number. Grammars follow and formulate custom; they neither precede nor dictate.

The inability of the grammarian to dictate to custom is made especially evident when we consider that thing more subtle than syntax and in composition no less important, which we call Idiom. That a writer shall be idiomatic is as essential to writing well as the avoidance of solecisms, yet every student of the language knows how elusive and difficult of attainment is a sound understanding of the idioms of any tongue.

An idiom is the personal—if the word may be allowed—the personal idiosyncrasy of a language. It is a method of speech wherein the genius of the race making the language shows itself as differing from that of all other peoples. What style is to the man that is idiom to the race. It is the crystallization in verbal forms of peculiarities of race temperament—perhaps even of race eccentricities.

It is customary to define an idiom as the form of language which cannot be translated into another tongue; and the example which is commonly given is the habit English-speaking peoples have of saying: "You are right," whereas the Latin form—literally translated—would be: "You speak rightly," the French: "You have reason," and the German: "You have right." An idiom is independent of grammatical rules,—sometimes is in distinct violation of them. It makes us say: "A ten-foot pole," "A two-dollar bill," "A five-acre lot,"—where a plural adjective modifies a singular substantive, or to speak more accurately is compounded with it. It decides that we shall write: "More [friends] than one friend has told me,"—although the subject of "told" is "friends" understood. An idiom boldly ignores the derivation of words. Since "circumstances" means "things standing around," it is evidently logical to use the phrase, "in these circumstances." The genius of the language decides that the form shall be, "under these circumstances;" and whoever writes "in" for "under" not only uses unidiomatic English, but lays himself open to the charge of pedantry. Untranslatable and above rules, Idiom is as inviolable as the laws of the Medes and the Persians, and for him who sins against it there is no pardon.

For idioms there is no law save that of Good Use, and perhaps in the discernment of no other rules is required so critical and so nice a discrimination. English which is not idiomatic becomes at once formal and lifeless, as if the tongue were already dead and its remains embalmed in those honorable sepulchres, the philological dictionaries. On the other hand, English which goes too far, and fails of a delicate distinction between what is really and essentially idiomatic and what is colloquial, becomes at once vulgar and utterly wanting in that subtle quality of dignity for which there is no better term than distinction. The grammarian, moreover, wageth against Idiom a warfare as bitter as it is unceasing. It is distinctly idiomatic to use in certain cases what is known as the "flat adverb,"—the adverb in the adjective form without *ly*. The man who writes "speak loudly," "speak more loudly," "speak plainly," "walk fastly," "drink deeply," "speak lowly," "the moon shines brightly," "the sun shines hotly," may have the applause of grammarians and his own misguided conscience, but he is not writing idiomatic English. His virtue must be its own reward, since he can never win the approval of lovers of sound, wholesome, living English. Those who use the language idiomatically write "speak loud," "speak louder," "speak plain," "walk fast," "drink deep," "speak low," "the moon shines bright," and "the sun shines hot." Yet these idiomatic distinctions are often very delicate. An adverb is sometimes properly used in its flat form with an imperative when in other cases the form in *ly* is proper. We say, for instance, "walk slow, walk slower;" but "He walked slowly across the field and more slowly over the bridge." Nothing but the careful training of the perceptions avails for distinctions such as these.

Another idiomatic construction against which the purist waggeth his tongue and gritteth his teeth is the ending of a sentence with a particle. Instead of the good old idiomatic "Where does it come from?" he would have us say "Whence does it come?" For "Where is it going to?" he offers "Whither is it going?" Both of his phrases are eminently respectable, but there is sometimes a lack of vitality in too eminent respectability! Do not be afraid to say: "The subject which I spoke to you about;" "The conclusion that we came to;" "The man whom I talked with;" "This is a cause to stand up for;" "It is worth living for;" "A name to conjure with;" and the allied phrases which would never have been tolerated for an instant if the language had been made in libraries instead of having grown up in the lives of peoples and on the tongues of breathing men.

Professor Reed, of the University of Pennsylvania, admirably says:—

The false fastidiousness which shuns a short particle at the end of a sentence is often fatal to a force which belongs to the language in its primal character.

He points out that only the misapplication of analogies from Continental languages has brought into discredit this characteristic English idiom. He quotes Bacon, "Houses are built to live in, and not to look on;" Donne, "Hath God a name to curse by?" and Burke, "The times we live in." He might have gone to contemporary authors, and cited Stevenson, "After expedients hitherto unthought of," "He was all fallen away and fallen in;" James, "The different bedrooms she has successively slept in," "There is almost literally nothing he does not care for;" Newman, "The elect are few to choose out of;" Lowell, "In accomplishing what he aimed at," "The words are chosen for their value to fill in," "The soil out of which such men as he are made is good to be born on, good to live on, good to die for and be buried in." It would not be difficult to extend the list until it should include all the writers of idiomatic English.

It is necessary, however, to add here a word of warning. Allowing a particle to come at the end of a sentence or clause because it belongs there idiomatically is one thing; letting the particle drag loosely along behind from a lack of skill or energy sufficient to manage the construction properly is quite another. Idiom is a cloak which may be made to cover as many vices as virtues. The beginning and end of clause or sentence are the emphatic parts, and to give the close to an unimportant word is to waste an opportunity and weaken the effect of the whole. The reason why the idiomatic final particle is permissible is because it really belongs to the emphatic idea or is practically a part of the verb which precedes it. In the phrase "the times we live in," it is evident that "in" is in intention part of the idea expressed by the verb, so that the sentence does not close with the particle "in" but with the verb "live in;" and so on for the other examples which have been quoted.

A common instance of unidiomatic use of a particle at the end of a sentence is that of closing with the sign of the infinitive. "Do as you have a mind to" is bad English because the words "mind" and "to" do not in idea belong together. Either the verb should be expressed,—"Do as you have a mind to do," or the sentence should be recast. However strong colloquial precedent may seem, do not allow that forlornly orphaned sign of the infinitive to come trailing along alone as a last word.

The idiomatic use of conjunctions is one mark of a finished and careful style. It is perhaps too much to say that if a writer takes care of his particles the other parts of speech will take care of themselves, but it is at least true that no style can be lucid and polished in which the particles—and especially the conjunctions—have not been looked to most carefully. Amateur writers are apt to seem aware of the existence of only two conjunctions, " and" and "but;" while they are especially careful to omit the conjunction "that." It has been remarked that one of the important means by which the French masters secure that wonderful clarity and vivacity of style which so few English authors have been able to approach is a careful and explicit discrimination of the value of connectives. A stylist might be not very inaccurately defined as a writer who is always conscientious in his choice of conjunctions. Coleridge's remarks on this point have often been quoted:—

A close reasoner and a good writer in general may be known by his pertinent use of connectives. Read that page of Johnson; you cannot alter one conjunction without spoiling the sense. It is in a linked strain throughout. In your modern books for the most part, the sentences in a page have the same connection with each other that marbles have in a bag; they touch without adhering.—*Table Talk*, May 15, 1833.

This is impatiently inexact, it may be, but the modern tendency, especially in careless newspaper work, is to do away with connectives for the sake of securing briskness. The result is abruptness always and confusion generally. Insignificant as they seem, connectives are the articulations of the skeleton of a composition, and unless they be flexible and delicately adjusted there is no possibility of freedom of movement in the whole.

Certain weak idioms which are common in conversation are apt to creep into the writings of those not over sensitive to literary effects, but these colloquialisms are religiously avoided by careful writers. An example of this sort of thing is the detestable use of "got"—as a substitute for "have" or as a superfluous appendage to it,—which is so conspicuous a vice in England. In America this is at least theoretically frowned upon, and indeed it is protested against by the best authorities on the other side of the water.

Of course I have not space to take up one by one all the idiomatic expressions of the language. These given will serve as examples, and I have but to add that there is perhaps no better way of becoming sensitive to idiom than by conversing with rustics and reading the English classics. Neither method is of value without the restraining and enlightening influence of sound good judgment, but the student who is able to criticise his own work and compare it with that of the masters will find the talk of country folk and the works of the old masters alike helpful in the formation of an idiomatic style.

The matter of long sentences or short sentences is practically the same as that of long or short words. The question is what effect the writer wishes to produce. If he desires to treat a subject with dignity, to impress by gravity of manner, or to produce a mood of solemnity or melancholy, it is all but essential that his sentences shall be long. If on the other hand it is his object to produce an effect of lightness, to induce a feeling of gayety, of briskness, to make the blood run swiftly in the veins, his style will be crisp with short sentences. With even a limited amount of literary training the choice of length in sentences becomes almost instinctive.

Something of the same principle is to be applied to sentences loose and sentences periodic. A loose sentence is one in which the meaning and the grammatic structure are complete at some point before the end; a periodic sentence is one in which sense and sentence end together. If I say, "We all praise periodic sentences, but few of us write them," I have given an example of the truth of the statement. The sense and the grammatic construction are both complete at the middle of the sentence. If this be rewritten so as to read, "Although we all praise periodic sentences, few of us write them," we have a periodic form in which sense and construction are alike incomplete until the close.

That closeness of structure which in an inflected language is imparted by the form of words must in English depend upon word arrangement; and from this it follows that the question of making the sentence periodic must be subordinate to the matter of bringing the right words together. The tendency of the language is toward a loose structure; but between the two sorts of sentences that we are considering there is the difference that there is between giving to a person a thing in pieces and giving it to him whole. In the loose sentence you present to him one portion after another, often in a way which leaves him uncertain at the end of the different parts whether there is or is not more to come; in the periodic, you offer to him the whole at once. Evidently the latter is the more definite, the more precise, the more finished. It is, however, so often impossible to make a sentence periodic without apparent effort that no style could be wholly periodic without seeming elaborately and even painfully studied; hence as a matter of fact all good style consists of a judicious mingling of the two kinds of sentence.

The danger in a style too uniformly periodic is that of appearing stiff and formal; and it seems to be true that the best and most flexible

English contains a larger portion of loose sentences than of periodic. Reaching out my hand for volumes which chance to be within arm's length of my writing-table, I find that of the first fifteen sentences in Lowell's essay on Chaucer, ten are loose and five periodic; of the same number at the beginning of Henry James' essay on Balzac, nine are loose and six periodic; at the commencement of Stevenson's paper on Burns the loose are to the periodic eight to seven; Saintsbury's essay on De Quincey begins with the same proportions; while that by the same author on Sydney Smith opens with thirteen loose relieved but by two periodic. Of course such examples are not conclusive, but they are at least illustrative.

In all these matters the important thing is to train one's self to do whatever it seems well to do, by the use of the form most apt for the effect desired. Since the natural tendency of the untrained writer is towards loose sentences, it is well to conquer the art of writing periodically. In this, as in all points of the study of composition, the thing aimed at is to be able to do with language whatever is desired; to become as absolutely master of it as the cunning sculptor is master of the modeling-clay, which is as plastic under his hand as if it were a part of his very thought.

V

Principles of Quality

When an architect builds a palace, or an edifice no matter how much humbler, he first attends to the unity, the proportions, and to the strength of the structure; after that he has to consider the harmony, the finish, and the adornment. According to the nature and purpose of the building, it may be given a coat of mineral paint, such as that which made the transient fortune of Silas Lapham, it may be set with clustering statues like an Old World cathedral, or it may be jeweled with precious marbles and flower-bright mosaics like the Taj Mahal.

The analogy between this process and that of the writer is close enough to excuse the somewhat florid comparison. First is to be considered the mechanical form of what is written; unity, proportion, and texture must be looked to, and afterward there must be thought of the harmony, finish, and adornment. When we have studied the Principles of Structure,—Unity, Mass, and Coherence,—we have next to do with the Principles of Quality.

Whatever work interests a reader may be said to touch him in one of three ways: it may appeal to his understanding, to his emotions, or to his imagination. In other words, it may affect him by its intellectual, by its emotional, or by its imaginative or æsthetic quality. Bearing in mind that any nomenclature is a matter of convenience, and that we use names chiefly as a means of dividing the subject into portions which may be handled less awkwardly than the whole, we may call these three qualities Clearness, Force, and Elegance.

If we examine our feelings in regard to anything which we read, we find that it has been easily intelligible, or that it has bothered our comprehension; it has interested us, stirred us, or has left us indifferent or bored; and it has or has not produced in us a sense of beauty and elevation of mood. Neither these sensations nor the qualities which produce them are sharply separable; but the distinctions perceptibly exist, so that for purposes of study the qualities may conveniently be treated one at a time. It is easy to see that in understanding the meaning of a thing we most markedly use the intellectual faculties; that in liking or disliking we respond to an appeal to the emotions; and that in feeling beauty and appreciating the æsthetic, we necessarily employ the imagination. The first is a question of comprehension; the second of feeling; and the third of taste. Clearness is the intellectual principle of style; Force the emotional; and Elegance the æsthetic.

The Principles of Structure must precede and underlie those of Quality. Speaking broadly, we may say that it is idle to attempt to give to a composition or to a sentence Clearness, Force, or Elegance, unless it is already satisfactory in Unity, Mass, and Coherence. The closest attention to the laws of mechanical form, however, is not sufficient to secure quality. For the secret of that it is needful to go further.

It is in Clearness that the Principles of Quality are most obviously associated with those of Structure. If an author has carefully considered the Unity of his composition, if he has massed it properly in parts and as a whole, if he has looked well to its Coherence,—it is hardly possible that he should fail of being readily understood. Close attention to the mechanics of style will generally make a writer intelligible, provided always that he wishes his meaning to be apprehended easily, and that he himself knows what he is attempting to say.

These two considerations are of much practical importance. Sometimes writers do not choose to be clear. George Meredith seems often to write with the deliberate intention of forcing the reader to go slowly,—as if from the feeling that what can be read rapidly is in danger of being merely skimmed over. There are others, like Thomas Carlyle, who deliberately obscure what they write, apparently in the hope of adding by complexity an air of mystery to commonplaces and a meretricious dignity to wisdom.

Take, for instance, this sentence:—

If for the present, in our Europe, we estimate the ratio of Ware to Appearance of Ware so high even as One to a Hundred (which, considering the Wages of a Pope, Russian Autocrat, or English Game-Preserver, is probably not far from the mark),—what almost prodigious saving may there not be anticipated, as the Statistics of Imposture advances, and so the manufacture of Shams (that of Realities rising into clearer and clearer distinction therefrom) gradually declines, and at length becomes all but wholly unnecessary!—Carlyle: *Sartor Resartus*, ii. 3.

Here the lack of lucidity is intentional. The author has sacrificed it to the particular effect which he wished to produce. He sought to give to what he wrote an air of bizarre and piquant individuality, and it is for this that he so distorts and convulses his sentences. The purpose is as conscious as that which informs the gyrations of an acrobat. There is the same relation between a page of "Sartor Resartus" or the "French Revolution" and a page of ordinary prose that there is between the marvelous distortions of a contortionist and the walk of a gentleman,—each, of course, being well in its place.

Compare with the sentence just given, this passage from an undergraduate's theme:—

Chaucer's influence on the language was great, and he helped to put the language before the people in a way that had not been done before, so that it is evident that there was a great result from this. This was because he helped to change the English language, and in this way he was very influential in affecting the language.

Here an unhappy youth, engaged in all but mortal combat with an examination paper, was endeavoring to say something when he had nothing to say. Of course he could not but fail, since it is impossible to show clearly what one does not see clearly.

With these put also this, which again is from an undergraduate's theme:—

If the student respects a professor, as many do, he can show his respect in many ways; if he does not, and there are teachers who do not command the respect of students (I do not consider the question to be confined to this school, and in some colleges there are men on the Faculty who are not respected, nor do they deserve to be) and I think a man should raise his hat only to ladies or to gentlemen that have ladies with them.

Here the writer knew fairly well what he wished to say, although he had not taken the trouble to think it out very sharply. His difficulty was that he lacked technical skill in expression.

These examples illustrate the causes from which obscurity may arise. The first is legitimate. Whether we agree that Carlyle or George Meredith or Browning has carried obscurity beyond the farthest limit at which it is permissible has nothing to do with the fact that there are times when it is the right of an author to sacrifice Clearness to some other effect which he seeks. It is, however, fair to say that in ordinary experience these emergencies are pretty nearly as rare as the appearance of white blackbirds; and that at least no writer has a right to discard Clearness until he has secured it. Certainly no one can successfully employ obscurity as a means of producing literary effect until he has acquired the art of writing with transparent simplicity.

Of the second cause it is sufficient to say here that no outward aid can enable the student to overcome it. To think sharply and lucidly is the result of self-discipline. It is a matter of mental exercise, and while a student may be sent to a mental as to a physical gymnasium, all strengthening of the mind as of the muscles must be the result of individual exertion. There has as yet been discovered no system of intellectual *massage*, by means of which the understanding may attain to the benefits of work without doing anything.

While rules or wise maxims help little in this matter of mental clearness, it is a thing so important and so universally essential in all intellectual training that it is difficult to pass it without a word more. If a new Dante were to people a new Inferno with sinners guilty of crimes intellectual, as the stern old Florentine peopled his with those who violated moral laws, the most populous circle would be devoted to those who mistakenly think themselves to think. There is a discouragingly large portion of mankind whose mental processes are apparently those of the oyster. They are mentally so indolent or incapable that the labor of reflecting is entirely beyond them. No student can afford to remain in doubt as to whether he really thinks, or merely indulges in vague mental impressions which are to genuine thought as is the dull smouldering of a heap of wet leaves in a November fog to a brisk beech-wood fire on a wide hearth in a winter night.

Macaulay is right when he says: "Propriety of thought and propriety of diction are commonly found together…. Obscurity of expression generally springs from confusion of ideas." He might have added that it is of great importance that the writer be able to think of his subject as a whole. It is easy for the mind to grasp a small thing and it is proportionately harder for it to seize upon a greater; yet upon the power to hold work in the mind in its entirety must as surely depend success in writing as does all vigorous mental development.

The third cause of obscurity, inability to express the thought which one has, is at once the most common, and the most inexcusable. Here we are dealing with a tangible thing, to a great extent a matter of rule, and, at most, largely a question of study. There is no reason why a person of ordinary intelligence should not be able to express whatever he is able to think. Indeed, whoever has fully thought out an idea has already phrased it, and if he has even a moderate amount of training in composition should have no difficulty in expressing it on paper if he will but take the necessary pains.

It is evident that what is clear to one reader may be obscure to another. It follows that the first question to be decided is to what audience a composition is to be addressed. Few of us can understand this sentence from a treatise on comparative embryology.

The inner wall of each of the paired cavities forms a splanchnopleuric mesoblast, and the outer wall of the whole the somatic mesoblast.

This is clear to readers who understand the technical language of embryology; and for them the author wrote. Parallel examples might be given which would show how many sorts of writing there are which are clear to a limited audience only. The reports of base-ball games are unintelligible to the average English reader, while to the American the notes on cricket are equally meaningless. The criticisms of artists upon pictures seldom convey a definite impression to those not versed in the technical language of painting; and the same principle holds throughout all sorts of literature.

The whole matter then resolves itself into the simple maxim: Use the language of those addressed. There is somewhere a story of a lady who always spoke to her maid in French, because in taking the situation the girl had wrongfully claimed to know that tongue. The mistress held stubbornly to the position that the maid should understand, and she endured the discomforts of never being well served rather than abandon it. Much writing and not a little talking is all but as absurd. Constantly authors address themselves to the general public in language which they know or might know the general public will not understand. Whatever else the human race may be, it is not logical; there are few of us free from the fault of sometimes acting upon assumptions which we know to be false; and nowhere is this fact more strikingly illustrated than in composition.

This question of using the language of those addressed is one which meets every teacher at the very threshold of the class-room. The best instructor is not he who knows most, but he who imparts most; and he imparts most who most perfectly speaks the language of his pupils. It is of no use daily to fire over the heads of children all the wisdom of Solomon if it be embodied in a language which is not theirs. The teacher who really teaches does not take the attitude of the lady whose maid should have known French; he does not assume that pupils should understand what he says; he simply considers whether as a matter of fact they do understand. If they do not, he sets himself with patience to re-phrase it, and, if need be, re-phrase again, until he has put it into language which the children cannot fail to comprehend. It is not a question of what might be understood but of what must be. It is true that this calls for a patience which is almost divine, and there are teachers in the common schools to-day who are only preserved to us because the age of translation to heaven is past. There are unhappily others who do not understand that this patient and laborious seeking after the intellectual dialect of the pupil is the only possible means of imparting instruction; and thus it happens that some schools are taught in a language which, while it is English, is yet hardly more intelligible to the students than would be Choctaw or the speech of Borrioboola-Gha.

In writing, the safest guide in this respect is sound, homely common sense. Write without nonsense in the way of self-consciousness or affectation. Make it always a rule in general composition to aim at the simple, average man; to write so that the traditionally foolish wayfaring man need not err therein. Remember that the aim is not to write so that one may be understood, but to write so that one cannot be misunderstood.

Absurdly enough, human vanity comes in here. Untrained writers are apt to feel that they lower themselves if they condescend to write for the intellectual bourgeoisie. Many a clever young author has come to grief because he could not bring himself to use simple language lest it should seem that he had not command of a more elaborate diction. He has failed because he could not be willing to address the ordinary reader lest he thereby might appear to show that he had not the gift of speaking to the learned. The great writers are men who are free from this weakness; who are intent upon making their message understood, and not upon preserving a foolish appearance of superiority. Shakespeare did not disdain to write for the London apprentices brawling in the pit, or Homer to sing for semi-barbarians half-drunken at the feast. The masterpieces of literature which have been addressed to the educated few are revered; those which have been confessedly for the many have been read and lived upon. To take as instances two works written at about the same time: "Paradise Lost" has been commended by critics and admired by scholars; "Pilgrim's

Progress" has been and is the favorite book with thousands. The one has always been profoundly admired and the other has been loved. I do not mean that this is all that might be said of these classics, or that there are no other considerations in determining their worth, but they do serve to make more clear the fact that to reach the general reader it is necessary to write for the general reader.

Speaking the language of the average man includes also the confining of allusions to the range of his probable knowledge, the taking for granted nothing which he may not reasonably be supposed to know. The temptation to show erudition is at the elbow of every writer. When, near the beginning of this lecture, I referred in an easy manner to the Taj Mahal, I was instantly conscious that I had used the comparison with a pleasant sense of the air of superior knowledge which it might give. However it may be with you, the probabilities are that the ordinary reader would not be sufficiently familiar with the elaborate ornamentation of that wonder of the East to make my comparison to its jewelled walls effective, and I left it only because I wanted to use it here as an illustration.

It is no less needful to appeal to the average emotional experiences of mankind in order to be clear to the general reader. It must be remembered that all art is based on the assumption of a community of human feelings; in other words, upon the theory that the fundamental emotions are shared by all mankind. The more closely a writer holds to common humanity, to common human experience, the more wide will be the range of his work, and the more clear will he be in those very matters where clearness is most difficult of attainment. The more subtile and remote from ordinary human life are the emotions and the passions to be portrayed, the more absolute is the necessity of conveying them in terms of simple and common experience. Analyze one of the tragedies of Shakespeare or of the old Greek dramatists, and you will find that its tremendous effects are produced by means essentially simple. By keeping always within the range of the sympathies and feelings common to humanity, the masters are able to make every stroke tell; and this method is in the nature of things the only possible one. Common humanity can comprehend only what it has felt.

To gain Clearness it is necessary first to avoid all vagueness of thought and all vagueness of expression. It is needful to shun ambiguity of word or of phrase, and that more subtle ambiguity which may arise from ill-considered paragraphing, from misproportion, or from bad arrangement of the parts of a composition. It is no less important to write with a constant remembrance of the audience addressed; to use their language, and to appeal to the emotions and experiences which are likely to be common to the average individual of the class for which one writes. Inexperienced writers may make the mistake of supposing that this is the rule by which mediocrity is to be reached; but as a matter of fact these are the principles upon which have been written the masterpieces of the world.

VI

Principles of Quality Continued

Force has been defined as the quality which appeals to the emotions. Obviously, what we read interests us or it does not. Persons who are conscious that they are not qualified to judge of the value of work, yet who are secretly convinced that their judgment must be of value despite this fact, are rather apt to take refuge in the annoying phrase, "I am no judge, but I can tell what I like." Even this qualified statement is often conspicuously untrue, but in so far as they really can tell what they like, they are judges of the force of what they read, their own emotions being the standard; and in so far as they can tell why they like or fail to like, they are judges also of the means by which force has been secured, or for want of which it has been lost.

We are accustomed to associate with the term which is here used a signification more narrow and more intense than that which is given to it in this connection. Generally, when we speak of a piece of literature as having force, we mean that it has the power to move us to an unusual degree. We think at once of the cyclone-swept pages of Carlyle, of the penetrating mysteriousness of Kipling, or of the fate-pervaded realism of Hardy; at least, of something moving and intense. In discussing force as a quality of style, we must make the term wide enough to cover whatever power a literary composition has of arousing interest by what it is. An accidental circumstance—the antiquity of a book, the fact that it was written by a particular person, the part which it has played in an important event, and so on—might arouse a certain sort of interest in it, but this would have nothing to do with the force of the composition. Those things which certain magazines bring out, written by the notoriety of the hour,—the prize-fighter, the woman who has made herself most conspicuous in ways decent or indecent,—have not in themselves anything that can be called Force in the proper sense of the term. They may attract much attention, but it is by accidental circumstances, and not by their quality.

"The secret of Force," Mr. Wendell writes, "is connotation;" and he goes on to exemplify this thus:—

> Compare these three simple statements: "I found him very agreeable one afternoon;" "I found him very agreeable one wet afternoon;" "I found him very agreeable one wet afternoon in a country house." Now all that the word "wet" says is that the afternoon was watery; but it clearly implies that it was an afternoon when you would not care to be out of doors. All that the words "in a country house" state is a simple fact of locality; but they imply that you were in a place where not to be out of doors was probably a serious trial to the temper. So the last statement as a whole, "I found him very agreeable one wet afternoon in a country house," suggests, though it does not state, that the person spoken of was one whose charms could overcome a pretty bad temper. At the same time it is a phrase which I fancy anybody would admit to hold the attention more strongly than either of its predecessors; and its superiority in force lies not so much in the bare facts which it adds to the first statement as in the thoughts and emotions it suggests. Still again, take this sentence from one of M. de Maupassant's stories: "It was the 15th of August—the feast of the Holy Virgin, and of the Emperor Napoleon." He states only two facts about the 15th of August, and these in the simplest of words. Neither by itself would hold one's attention enough to remain long in memory. But put them together; think what the Holy Virgin means to Catholic Europe, and what the Emperor Napoleon means to those who are not subdued by the magic genius of Bonaparte,—and you have a sentence that when mid-August comes about will hover in your head. Yet the force of this—so greatly superior to the force of either statement by itself—lies not in what is actually said, but wholly in what is implied, suggested, connoted, in this sudden, unexpected antithesis.

The thing which the writer has caused the reader to think—or even to suppose himself to think—is sure to interest him. The dullest of bores is absorbed in his own words, and in effect that which the reader receives by suggestion is his own thought. What is denoted is the word of the writer; what is connoted is for the time being the thought of the reader.

It is not difficult to see that Clearness is an aid to Force; or, to put it more exactly, that a lack of Clearness will interfere with Force. Yet the one is by no means essential to the other. The diction of "The Ordeal of Richard Feverel," that book so strong that it wrings the heart almost like a fierce personal sorrow, is in passages so obscure as to have given rise to the rather cheap *mot* that the novel would be successful if it were translated into English. Almost any page of Carlyle might also be cited in illustration; while that Clearness may fail to secure Force is proved by the pellucidly stupid lucubrations of an innumerable company of authors whom nobody could fail to understand if it were possible to keep awake to read them.

Connotation may be the result of various causes. It may be produced by a swiftness and briskness of motion which so awakens and quickens the mind that the reader is aroused to thought, and seizes each idea presented as if he had himself originated it. It is this sort of force that we mean when we speak of the vivacity or the brilliancy of a work. The secret lies chiefly in passing quickly from one significant point to another. This involves, it is apparent, the power of selecting the significant, and of bringing this out while avoiding the unessential.

The effectiveness of the sensational story depends largely upon a quality closely allied to this, although here it is a matter not so much of style as of material. The tale which moves rapidly from situation to situation, so that the reader seems to share the adventures of the characters, often owes as much to the swiftness of its progress as to the nature of the story told. It owes more, as a general thing, to the vividness with which the exciting situations are imagined and presented. The more real a thing seems to the reader, the more suggestive it must be to him, and the more likely is he to share the sensations set down, so that for the moment it seems as if he were actually experiencing them. In other words, the more real the narrative, the more suggestive it becomes.

One great means of producing this sense of reality either in narrative or in any other kind of composition, whether in the setting forth of thoughts, or in the telling of events, is in making what is written specific. The specific term is apt to be more suggestive than the general from the fact that it presents to the mind an idea which can be grasped readily. When one reads that the Indians are on the war-path and are ravaging the country, one has a vague feeling of horror; but if one is told that the Red Men have crossed the bounds of Big Lick Reservation, have murdered and scalped a settler named John Thing, have burned his cabin, and carried off his wife and children, there is no vagueness about it. The impression becomes at once vivid and forceful in what it denotes, and stirring in what it connotes.

It is from a misapplication of this fact that modern fiction has fallen into that vice which has been known as Realism—perhaps because it is less real than any other sort of fiction ever devised. It is apparently by a perception of the effectiveness of the specific, that Realists have been led into the error of believing in the effectiveness of the minute.

Before leaving the quality under discussion it is well to say a word about what is called "reserved force." Our respect for a writer is always increased by feeling that he might do more than he is doing. We are led on by a desire to see what greater things he will accomplish. The feeling in reading an author who is evidently doing his utmost is not unlike that felt in crossing a bridge which shakes with the footfall. It may carry us over the stream, but on the other hand it may break under us. I once heard a lady explain her dislike for a certain youth by saying: "I never could endure a man who is always doing his darnedest!" The expression is unhappily vulgar, but it does seem to me to be humanly expressive. We do not like to feel that we have come to the end of the resources of a friend or of an author.

How then does a writer produce an impression of reserved force? The phrase meets one in book reviews, and to inexperienced writers is apt to convey little but bewilderment. One way in which the finished literary craftsman secures the impression of reserved power is by deliberately making the minor parts of his work weaker than those more important. In other words, he gains the effect of reserved strength by reserving strength. Often it is well in the revision of a composition to lessen the stress of expression in unimportant passages; to soften down, as it were, all portions except the high lights. The natural tendency of every earnest writer is to express himself as vigorously as possible, and in the first draft this is well,—provided always that he has the self-control and the skill so to modify in revision the less important parts that the emphasis shall be properly proportioned. Shading in literature is a matter which it is not easy to explain without examples much longer than it is possible to use here. It must be learned by the study of masterpieces. It is well to keep in mind, however, that it is oftener the result of a clever softening of minor passages than of a heavier emphasis upon important portions; and above all that the secret of shading and of reserved force as well is proportion. It is rather comparative than absolute stress which is effective. Vehemence is not vigor. Make up your mind clearly what points you wish to bring out most sharply; that is half of the process: then see to it that the remaining parts of the composition are kept subordinate to these; that is the rest of it.

Largely, too, is a sense of reserved force imparted by smoothness and ease of style. A style which is rough generally seems hard and labored. To carry the reader forward easily seems to be to carry him surely, and gives the impression that the writer could go faster and farther if he but chose.

One of the secrets of smoothness is the art of easy transition from one paragraph to another, from one sentence to another, from one thought to another. In Macaulay's essay on "Machiavelli," for instance, after speaking of the correspondence of the Italian, the author continues:

It is interesting and curious to recognize, in circumstances which elude the notice of historians, ... the fierce and haughty energy which gave dignity to the eccentricities of Julius; the soft and graceful manners which masked the insatiable ambition and the implacable hatred of Cæsar Borgia.

We have mentioned Cæsar Borgia. It is impossible not to pause for a moment on the name of a man in whom the political morality of Italy was so strongly personified, etc.

And so the essayist goes on to draw a comparison between Cæsar Borgia and Machiavelli, which he had of course intended from the first, but which he has had the art to introduce as if it were a sudden thought. The effect is as if the name of Borgia had suggested the parallel; and not only does this give an air of spontaneity, but it also impresses the reader with a feeling of security in the resources of the writer. If the mere mention of a famous name can bring so much from his mind, it is evident that that mind must be most abundantly stored.

More subtle, and therein so much the more admirable, is the art which links together the parts of a composition simply by closeness of meaning. To illustrate it would take too much room, but all the great essayists afford examples, and it is in them that this detail of literary skill may most conveniently be studied.

Another matter closely connected with Force is that of beginning and ending well. If the opening sentence of a composition interest the reader he is ready to go on, while an effective close leaves him with a pleasant impression of what he has been reading. In a composition divided into parts or chapters, it is especially important to see to it that the separate portions end effectively. The general verdict upon a book is largely made up of the sum of impressions received from the endings of sections. Here again the reader will find examples in all the masters, but a few may be given. In a vein almost familiar, but in entirely good taste, Lowell begins his superb essay on Chaucer:—

Will it *do* to say anything more about Chaucer? Can any one hope to say anything, not new but even fresh, on a topic so well worn?

This very statement of the difficulty provokes the reader to go on to see how that difficulty is overcome.

In somewhat the same vein is Saintsbury's beginning of his paper on Hogg:—

"What on earth," it was once asked, "will you make of Hogg?" I think that there is something to to be made of Hogg, and that it is something worth making.

Or take the opening of Stevenson's "Gossip on Romance:"—

In anything fit to be called by the name of reading, the process itself should be absorbing and voluptuous; we should gloat over a book, be rapt clean out of ourselves, and rise from the perusal, our minds filled with the busiest, kaleidoscopic dance of images, incapable of sleep or continuous thought.

The intoxication of the ideal which this gives us is so full of suggestion, it brings up so vividly the best delights that have marked our reading, that our minds are awake and alert from the start. We are not only ready but eager to go forward under the guidance of an author who has so charming a conception of what sort of a treat he should strive to give the reader.

Endings are if possible even more important, and they are carefully studied by masters of style. Take this conclusion of Lowell's "Abraham Lincoln:"—

Never was funeral panegyric so eloquent as the silent looks of sympathy which strangers exchanged as they met that day. Their common manhood had lost a kinsman.

One puts down the book with that suggestively solemn phrase sounding on in the brain like the reverberation when a great bell ceases its knell for a hero.

Or re-read the brief description of the tombstone of Hester Prynne, which closes "The Scarlet Letter," and which ends with a phrase so haunting:—

It bore a device, a herald's wording of which might serve for a motto and brief description of our now concluded legend, so sombre is it, and relieved only by one ever-glowing point of light gloomier than the shadow: "On a field, sable, the letter A, gules."

Or take the wonderful ending of that chapter in "Vanity Fair" which gives a description of Waterloo, and in a single sentence shows its relation to the story and brings the tale into closest connection with all of history and all of human life:—

The darkness came down on field and city, and Amelia was praying for George, who was lying on his face, dead, with a bullet through his heart.

It is of course unnecessary to go on with examples. The student can find them abundantly for himself. The point is that in his own work he shall remember to look carefully to this detail, since there is no single matter more closely connected with the effect of a composition.

It is evident that the power to interest and to arouse by suggestion must depend largely upon the extent to which the writer is able to enter into the reader's mood. In other words, that writer is most effectively suggestive who is most completely and practically sympathetic. The foundation of whatever is really vital must be in the genuine feeling and the actual experience of the author. This experience, it is true, may be actual in the imagination only, but it must have been felt as a reality. The secret of sympathy is in the well-known line of Sidney:—

"Fool," said my muse to me, "look in thy heart and write!"

It is idle to hope to hold any reader, or to move him strongly, unless we are really interested ourselves; and it is equally impossible to touch him if there be any suspicion on his part that we are not dealing with him with perfect frankness. What we write must be real to us, and it must be told with perfect frankness, if we are to reach the hearts of those we address.

There is perhaps no advice more wholesome for young writers than that they confine themselves absolutely to their own experience whenever it is in any way possible. If an illustration is to be given, a figure employed, a comparison used, let the illustration, the figure, the comparison be found in the things of which the writer has actual knowledge. It is not alone that this will insure a vitality which is hardly to be imparted to anything taken at second hand, but, what is of more importance, it will also make it at least more probable that the writer keeps within the experiences of his readers. Of the things which one has actually seen and felt, it is easy to judge how far they are usual; and the more closely a writer confines himself to usual things, the more forceful his style is likely to be.

A remark of Lowell's contains by implication a hint which we shall do well to notice here.

What he [Dryden] valued above all things was force, though in his haste he is willing to make shift with its counterfeit, effect.—*Dryden.*

The word "force" is here used in the sense of vigor and lasting power, its meaning being somewhat more limited than that in which we are using it as a technical term. It is the same in essentials, however, and the distinction which is brought out in the sentence quoted is one not to be overlooked. Effect is the transient, whereas force is the permanent: effect startles, force holds; effect is the sham, force the true. The worst type of style which sacrifices force to effect is the sensational novel, or the so-called "breezy" journalism. To startle, to shock, to produce a sensation, at whatever sacrifice of probability, of reason, or of good taste,—the thing is unfortunately too well known to need particularization.

An effeminate form of striving for effect is what is known as "fine writing." "Fine writing" is a fault so gross that it is not necessary to waste many words on it. It need only be said that there is no more certain indication of a hopelessly diseased literary taste, or of a hopelessly depraved habit of composition, than this absurdly antiquated verbal vice. Of course no writer who produces literature is guilty of it, but I somewhere have picked up an example which so happily illustrates all that could be said on the subject that I cannot forbear to quote it. It is from a novel called "Barabbas," by Miss Marie Corelli, and is part of the description of the appearance of Christ before Pontius Pilate. Water having been brought, Pilate, according to Miss Corelli, thus proceeded:—

Slowly lowering his hands, he dipped them in the shining bowl, rinsing them over and over again in the clear, cold element, which sparkled in its polished receptacle like an opal against the fire.

The Bible finds it possible to say all of this that is necessary in the words:—

Pilate took water, and washed his hands.

Miss Corelli's ingenuity in expanding and distorting has won its reward,—her novel has been warmly commended by Queen Victoria.

Even really great writers are not always free from this fault, although here it is apt to be from some mixture of humorous intent that they fall into it. Instead of "she hardened her heart," George Meredith writes, in one of those irritating sentences which are too frequent in his books, and which affect one like freckles on the face of a goddess, "She turned her inward flutterer to steel."

Force, then, depends upon suggestion, and this is secured by sincerity, by appeals to human experiences common to all, by freedom from affectations, and by attention to such details as proper beginnings and endings. Other means of securing it we shall deal with later. Here it is enough to insist again that the great secret of Force lies in earnestness, sincerity, and sympathy.

To pass from Force to Elegance is to advance from the more subtle to the most subtle. It is not difficult to be definite in speaking of Clearness; it is less easy in discussing Force; while, at the very outset of the consideration of Elegance, we are met by the fact that it is hardly possible even to define this third principle of quality. Indeed, it is perhaps not too much to say that nobody is even fully satisfied with this name for the æsthetic quality. "Elegance" is the term which is coming to be accepted as, on the whole, the most convenient and satisfactory offered; but I suppose that nobody would feel inclined to insist strongly upon this especial word. Mr. Wendell writes:—

Elegance is that distinguishing quality of style that pleases the taste; ... the æsthetic quality of style, that subtle something in a work of literary art which makes us feel delight in workmanship. Beauty, some call it; charm, others; others still, grace, ease, finish, mastery.

The name does not much matter; the quality matters greatly. It is this more than all else that gives lasting value to literature. There is in style an indefinable power of reaching the emotions of the reader which is beyond the effect of what is actually said, even beyond the effect of what is suggested. The quality which makes intelligible actual statement is Clearness; that which brings home to the reader the wealth of suggestion which may lie behind what is directly said is Force; while beyond both is that quality of style which conveys the intangible, which carries to the mind of the reader emotions too delicate to be confined in words, which touches and arouses as fineness of color or line or sound moves us in painting or sculpture or music. This is what we mean by Elegance. It is the æsthetic effect produced purely by the literary form; by the perfection of the relation between the end sought and the means employed; by the complete mastery of technique, and the employment of all the resources of art for the embodiment of the imaginative in literary form.

I am aware that my definition may make the matter less clear rather than more plain, but the thing is too elusive to be caught in the trap of a simple definition. Elegance is the quality in which the imagination most directly makes itself manifest. It is the most tangible proof that a writer possesses that power which at the start we spoke of as inborn and incommunicable. As a matter of workmanship, and so far as it may be learned, Elegance is chiefly the ability to convey in words the mood of the writer. It depends largely upon an exquisite sensitiveness to the indirect effect of words and of word-combination. It is to be cultivated by training the mind to consider always the value of terms in their connotation; to weigh them not only by their direct meaning, but by their association, and by the ideas and ideals and emotions which they bring to the mind; and by developing taste in literary construction. To write with Elegance, it is also necessary to keep in mind the effect upon the reader of the emotional word-color. The suggestions of words are dependent in part upon the mere vocal effect of the sounds producing them, upon the harmony of the sentence, the tone-value and cadence of clause and paragraph. All these things are elements which must be considered. Completely to master all these, so as to work upon the mind and imagination of the reader at will, is of course within the power of the great imagination only; but every student may advance toward it.

We are none of us able satisfactorily to define beauty, or to explain the pleasure which it excites; yet there is no one of us who has not recognized both. Why a curve is more pleasing to the eye than a straight line may be too deep a question; but none the less may one safely appeal to the universal experience that there are certain lines, certain forms, certain colors, certain sounds which give us pleasure. With equal assurance may one appeal to the universal instinct which is gratified by the adaptation of ends to means; to the innate human sense of the rightness of what is fitting; the constant pleasure in order, in appropriateness, in harmony. It is this instinct, this sense, this pleasure, which underlies the sensitiveness of the mind to what we call Elegance in composition.

The quality which we are discussing is, more than any other, dependent upon the personal taste and culture of the writer. The thing to be said to the student is perhaps this: "Elegance is the result of a keen and acutely imaginative perception of the fitness of things, and of a quick appreciation of beauty, with the power to convey both by a delicate adaptation of literary means to literary effects." A keen and acute perception of the fitness of things can only be acquired by the development of the taste. This is an affair of culture in its broadest sense, and it is hardly possible to separate here the question of literary excellence from that of general development. The study of the masterpieces of literature—always with earnestness and with sympathy—is the most direct means of improving a sensitiveness to literary fitness and to literary beauty. The adaptation of means to ends we shall go on considering throughout these talks; and now, as always, it is necessary to remember that the way to learn to write is to write. The way to achieve Elegance is to labor for it with that persistence which is in itself the best compensation which Heaven has bestowed upon man for all other boons denied. "Persistence, persistence, and persistence" is the motto which the student must engrave on his heart.

There will always remain the personal equation. No student can afford to close his eyes to the fact that all men are born intellectually unequal. To one has Nature given gifts of appreciation, of apprehension, and of expression, while from another she has withheld them. This personal difference affects all work, and it affects work more and more strongly as we draw nearer to that quality in literature which is incommunicable. Steadily, since the beginning of these talks, have we been advancing toward those fields of composition where comes into play that power which is the gift of the gods only; that imaginative essence which some men are dowered with at birth, and which some go seeking their whole lives through with insistence pathetically vain. The one thing important is, that the student not only accept his individual limitations, but that he do not stop short of them. It is necessary to realize that one has not genius, and then to work as if one had; and it is amazing how much may be done in this way. Nature, for instance, plainly intended that Matthew Arnold should not write elegant prose, and she absolutely forbade him to write poetry, yet he succeeded in doing both. The earnest student of literary art should resolutely refuse to be satisfied with any thing short of the miracle of the impossible, and haply so he may sometimes attain to it.

VII

Means and Effects

When the student has come to have a clear idea of what is to be sought in composition, he naturally goes on to inquire by what means a writer can gain the ends desired. It has been shown that there are certain principles which govern the mechanical structure of language, and also that there are as well principles which have to do with the quality of what is written. The next step is to examine the especial means which are at the command of the worker, and what effects may be secured by the use of given means.

It has already been said and insisted upon that it is necessary to know accurately what effect the writer desires to produce; and it is to be added that it is especially needful to realize from the start what is to be the conclusion of a work, great or small. The end of a composition is its consummation, the climax toward which all else conducts the reader, the ultimate effect to which all other effects are subordinate. The writer who sets out to go nowhere in particular, it has been said, is little likely to arrive anywhere. It is also to be remembered that, unless he is clearly aware what is to be his strongest point, he is not in a position to make all other parts properly subordinate to this,—to secure that careful proportion of emphasis which is one of the great essentials of all good work in whatever province of art.

Before he begins to write, the writer must make up his mind how he intends to end. He may, it is true, modify to some extent the first idea of the form in which this climax of his work is to be put, but it is safe to lay down as a general rule that he shall not essentially alter it. Whether one sits down to write a novel, a tale, an essay, an editorial, or a simple paragraph, let him know at least what the conclusion is to be, whether he is aware of the steps by which he is to reach this or not. The minor points may be thought up as one proceeds, but the end, which is in a manner the reason of the existence of the whole, must be clear in the mind of the writer from the very start.

It is this thing which Mr. Walter Pater means when he speaks of—

That architectural conception of a work which foresees the end from the beginning, and never loses sight of it, and in every part is conscious of all the rest, till the very last sentence does but, with undiminished vigor, unfold and justify the first.

The conclusion being well defined in the writer's thought, the next thing to be determined is the point of view. The point of view is to any composition what the hypothesis is to a proposition in geometry. It is the assumption of personality and of attitude which is presupposed from the start, and which must be rigidly maintained to the end.

If a writer is describing a landscape, he is obliged to fix in his own mind the point from which he is to consider that landscape as being seen,—whether near or remote, from hill or plain, from a bridge, a window, or it may be from the deck of a vessel. If he hopes to produce an impression which shall be clear, or to bring up vividly in the mind of the reader the thing described, he must not forget where the reader is supposed to be placed. If at the start he writes as if the view were remote, and then forgets and speaks of it as if it were near at hand, he destroys the consistency of the work and makes all ineffectual.

Another easily appreciated illustration is to be found in novels which are written in the form of an autobiography. Since the story is supposed to be narrated by one of the characters, it follows that nothing should be told which that person could not know. The introduction of scenes at which he could not have been present, of talk which he could not have heard, of thoughts which he had no means of discovering, completely dispels the illusion. If these things must be used, care must be taken to show how the narrator came to know them; since otherwise the hypothesis with which the author started is violated by the alteration of the point of view. The reader may or may not realize why the story loses its effect of reality, but he cannot fail to feel that it does lose it.

The same principle applies to everything that is written, even to the most trivial paragraph. Consciously or unconsciously, the writer at the start assumes a certain mental attitude toward the subject of which he writes, and this attitude he must carefully preserve. Of course the point of view may be progressive, as when one describes the scenery as viewed from a car window or shows the change of opinion; but in this case the motion is part of the original hypothesis. The first assumption must be adhered to, since to change the point of view is to break faith with the reader, and to break faith is to lose his confidence.

The philosophy of the matter is simple and obvious enough. It is the aim to induce the reader to submit, for the time being, his personality to that of the writer; to induce him to see with the eyes of the author, and to think with the author's mind. The slightest jar may destroy all illusion; the least difficulty may make the reader assert the supremacy of his own individuality. If even unconsciously his judgment is offended, his own consciousness is sure to assert itself, and he gives himself up no longer.

In practical work, the secret of preserving one mental attitude is largely that of being clearly aware of it. This detail of composition is perhaps most easily understood in its application to description or narration, but it must be as clearly realized in all composition. It is of high importance to determine beforehand what is the attitude of the writer both toward the subject and toward the reader addressed. The effect of a failure to observe this is found in a great many letters, and, perhaps I may be pardoned if I add, especially in feminine letters. The mind of woman is so flexible, so versatile, so capable of seeing many sides to a subject which to the duller masculine intellect seems to have but one, that it not infrequently happens that in a single page of a woman's letter there will be half a dozen points of view, or even that seeming impossibility of two or three points of view at once.

Often the application of this principle is so subtle that the tyro is entirely at a loss to know what is the matter with his sentence. Take these examples:—

The crowd turns, departs, disintegrates.

I noticed that the hat was of soft felt, and one might easily guess that it had been bought at a bargain sale. It lent a comfortable sense of satisfaction to its owner, and suggested to him the idea of going to church.

In the former, the writer's point of view is that of one looking out of a window at a crowd, and it is proper that he should say "turns, departs;" but after the crowd has departed he cannot see whether it disintegrates or not. If he should say, "Turns, disintegrates, departs," one could find no fault. In the second example, the point of view is at first that of an observer who sees the hat on the head of a stranger; then, without warning, it is shifted to the mind of any observer,— "one,"—and then, in a twinkling, to the thought of the wearer himself, which has been by the hat turned to the idea of going to church.

We shall have to do later with the point of view in its application to the various sorts of composition. Here it is enough to add the warning to inexperienced writers: Do not write to discover what you think, or how you feel about a subject. These questions are to be settled before writing is begun. In half the themes which I read, it is apparent that the writer has been going ahead in a sort of forlorn hope of ultimately learning his own opinions. To be in doubt when one begins, either of where one is bound or of how the attempt to get there is to be made, is as fatal in writing as in horse-racing. There is a good deal of what might be called the June-bug style of composition. Just as a beetle bangs his clumsy thick head against a window or a netting in hope that he may chance to strike a place where he can get through to the lamp within, so the June-bug writer goes banging absurdly down his page, bumping against any obstacle, trusting to fate and the chapter of accidents to show somewhere and somehow a way through. The man who has learned to write does not begin until he has an idea what his way through is to be. This being clear in his mind, he goes consistently toward it, and his consistency is what is called keeping the point of view.

The point of view being selected, it is often necessary to give the reader a clue to it. Sometimes it is needful to use no inconsiderable amount of skill to bring him to accept it. The well-trained reader always endeavors to put himself into complete sympathy with an author. The author is bound to make this as easy as possible, and even, if may be, to render it inevitable, to the end that the reader shall be forced to share the outlook of the writer, whether with conscious willingness or not. In obvious matters, like descriptions, the simple device of naming the point of view is enough. When Keats begins a poem,—

I stood tiptoe upon a little hill,—

he gives the point of view. So does Spenser when he opens the "Faerie Queene:"—

A gentle knight was pricking on the plain.

Equally is Lowell giving the point of view in the opening of the essay on Chaucer, already quoted: "Will it *do* to say anything more about Chaucer?" Here he at once puts the reader into the attitude of examining with fresh attention a subject which has been greatly discussed; by implication he intimates that there is still enough wheat in the often-threshed straw to make it worth while once more to turn it over. With equal skill and felicity he puts the reader into the mood in which he writes of Carlyle by the first sentence of another essay:—

A feeling of comical sadness is likely to come over the mind of any middle-aged man who sets himself to recollecting the names of the authors that have been famous, and the number of contemporary immortalities whose end he has seen since coming to manhood.

The reader perceives at once that the subject which is to be treated is to be regarded as of less assured permanence of importance than has been sometimes held. Evidently Lowell would not allude to the many transient so-called immortalities if he had not at least a suspicion that the contemporary reputation of Carlyle is likely to be lessened by time. The key-note is struck, and what follows is governed by it.

The secret of holding the reader to the point of view consists largely of keeping strictly to it in writing. If the author does not change his position, the reader is unconsciously drawn to it. There is a persuasive power in mere persistency which is recognized by any one who has had to do with an obstinate person, and this power tells in literature as fully as in domestic life.

We come next to figurative language, so called; and at this point it used to be the fashion to overwhelm the student with a list of dreadful names which was in itself enough to paralyze the mental processes, and to discourage at once and forever all aspiration after excellence. The appalling words *synecdoche, metonymy, antonomasia, asyndeton, anacolouthon, parrhesia, onomatopoeia,* and the rest, seemed to fascinate the soul of writers on composition as completely as they dazed and stupefied the understanding of the unhappy student. Pedants have amused themselves by darkening wisdom with words without knowledge, until it is all but impossible to come at anything practical in the old-fashioned books,—which were invariably called "treatises." It has been found that this is idle, and for the most part it has been laid aside. A few terms are for convenience still used, but in these days the effort, instead of being to give learned and pompous-sounding treatises on the art of composition, is if possible to set down what will assist the student in learning literary expression.

One of the first literary devices of which man's mind availed itself in its efforts to communicate ideas, was the use of figures. The thought moves naturally from the near to the remote, and from that which is known to that which is unknown. If we attempt to describe or explain a thing, we instinctively compare it to something which is familiar. "It is like this," we say; "it is similar to that thing which you know." It has often been remarked that all language is full of what Trench happily calls the fossil remains of metaphors,—words which were once used to convey an idea by comparing it to something known, but of which the figurative force is now forgotten. It is hardly necessary to give examples, because every student has had his attention called to this class of words; but their number illustrates how natural comparisons are, and how constantly they are called to aid expression.

To comparison it is customary to give two names, according as the likeness is stated explicitly or is implied. If a writer says, "The officer followed his victim like a sleuth-hound,"—a phrase which used to come into all the detective stories,—he makes an explicit comparison between the officer and a hound. If he writes, "The sleuth-hound of justice followed the track of his prey,"—a phrase still to be met with in newspapers of a certain class,—the comparison is the same, but it is assumed instead of being explicitly stated. To the expressed comparison is given the name "simile;" to the comparison assumed, the name "metaphor." It is of no great practical importance—unless in the line of encouraging carefulness in the discrimination of words— whether the distinction of names is carefully observed or not, but it is of some convenience in study.

The object of using figures is to add Clearness, or Force, or Elegance—or all of these—to the presentation of an idea. Constantly it happens that, by declaring that an unknown thing is like some known thing, the writer enables the reader to form an idea of it as it is. When in Job we read the beautiful simile, "My days are swifter than a weaver's shuttle," we are impressed by the passage of life with a vividness which could not be secured by any mere assertion, no matter how strong. The physical fact is so easily grasped that it makes more clear the intellectual reflection. In the same wonderful poem—and no one studying literature either for profit or for pleasure can afford to neglect the book of Job—there are beautiful figures enough to teach the art of using them were it otherwise forgotten. "Man is born unto trouble, as the sparks fly upward;" "I caused the widow's heart to sing for joy;" "The house appointed for all living;" "He maketh the deep to boil like a pot;" "Thou shalt come to thy grave in a full age, like as a shock of corn cometh in in his season,"—it is impossible not to see how in every case the thought is made more clear by the comparison.

It is evident, too, that in each case cited the expression has gained not only in Clearness but in Force. The moment a likeness is suggested, the mind of the reader is led to make the comparison, and is thus alive and alert; while in each case the figure suggests far more than any bare statement of fact. Since the secret of Force lies in connotation, in the suggestiveness which leads the mind onward into the mood so that it seems to itself to originate the ideas which are really given to it directly or indirectly by the author, it follows that in the use of figures is one of the most effectual means of securing this quality. Job says, "My days are swifter than a weaver's shuttle," and with the plain statement of the brevity of life come suggestions of the inevitableness of this brevity; we seem to see man tossed by the hand of the unseen, as a shuttle is thrown by the hand of the weaver, flung to and fro without power to stay or to resist. The whole despairing mood of the afflicted patriarch is summed up in the single simile. To come nearer to our own times, take that simile which is perhaps the most beautiful in English literature outside of Shakespeare:—

Fair as a star when only one

Is shining in the sky.

What is suggested is all the serenity of the eventide; the hush which comes between the daylight and the dark; the sense of peace; that feeling that a mystery is being wrought before our very eyes, when out of the faintly rose-purple haze of the sky throbs into radiance the first star. There is, too, that sense of restfulness that belongs to the twilight coolness, and, in some undefinable way, an idea of purity and innocence too high and too subtle to be defined. The gain in Force from such richness of suggestion is evident.

Even more closely than with Clearness or Force is the use of figures connected with Elegance. More than any other means at the disposal of the writer does this help to establish the mood which the author desires to share with his reader. More, perhaps, than any other means may figures be moulded to manifold uses, and thus they have large share in that adaptation of the means to an end, in which, as has been said, lies the secret of Elegance.

The proper use of figures is a thing which it is of the utmost importance for the student to master thoroughly; and I have ventured to set down a few rules which may be useful in practical work:—

1.   Never use a figure without a definite purpose, and never simply for its own sake.

2.   Never subordinate sense to figure.

3.   Make all figures easily comprehensible.

4.   Never make a comparison without realizing fully what it is.

5.   Never push a figure too far.

The reason for giving the first rule is, that so many young writers—I say young writers as a matter of courtesy, since there are plenty of old ones of whom it is no less true!—are given to the fault of piling up figures in much the same way that a tasteless milliner sometimes puts on her bonnets all the artificial flowers that can be made to stick to them, or as a stupid architect kills the design of a building by overloading it with ornaments. Figures exist for the style, and not the style for the figures; and from this follows not only the first rule, but the second also. To make the figure of more importance than the thing which it is to illustrate or to reinforce is to exalt the servant above the master.

The third rule is justified by the fact that figures are used to increase the lucidity of style, and that in a manner all comparisons are to be looked upon as in the nature of illustrations. It follows that they must, in order to fulfill their function, be easily understood themselves. Examine this passage:—

... The Wandering Jew has seen

Men come and go as the fixed Pyramids

Have seen even the steadfast polar star

Shift in its place.

To see any force in this, it is necessary to be aware that, since the Pyramids were built, the North Star has been altered in the precession of the equinoxes. A writer has no right to appeal to such special knowledge. This is one of the reasons why there are so few of the discoveries of modern science, rich and varied as they are, which can effectively be used in simile. The allusions would not be commonly understood. Another reason, equally potent, is that in general the connotation of scientific facts is too practical and uninspiring to add to the interest of poetic or imaginative themes. In old days it was the fashion for minor poets to go as far afield as possible for similes, which were dragged into verse as a Comanche Indian drags into camp his captives. Foot-notes were generously provided for the enlightenment of the reader, and nobody seemed to see the absurdity of illustrating a thought by a figure so obscure that it had itself to be explained. The tropes of the minor poets of the last century remind one of the remark of the Scotch goodwife about a learnedly obscure commentary on the Scriptures: "'Tis a braw wise book, na dout; an' the Bible does explain it wonderfu'." If a writer will hold to his own experience for his similes, he will have little difficulty in deciding what is likely to be readily understood by the general reader; and if he will remember that, provided that there be nothing vulgar or ludicrous or commonplace in its suggestion, the more homely an allusion the more effective it is likely to be, he cannot go far wrong.

The rule never to make a comparison without realizing fully what it is should be regarded as being as binding as a moral precept. If this be obeyed, there is no danger of the production of that hybrid microbe with which the pages of sensational fiction swarm, which is known as the mixed metaphor. I took up in the smoking-room of a steamer not long ago a novel called "Half a Million of Money," by Miss Amelia B. Edwards. I opened to a page on which was this sentence:—

> Trefalden cast a hasty glance about the room, as if looking for some weapon wherewith to slake the hatred that glittered in his eye.—Chap. xciv.

I give carefully the origin of this, since it seems like an absurd mock simile manufactured for the occasion. If the author had felt the force of the word "slake," and how it involves the idea of thirst, she could not have coupled it with "weapon" or with "glittered in his eye." A thirst which is slaked with a sword and glitters in the eye needs only to be realized to be cast aside.

Goethe, in speaking of Klopstock, once said:—

An ode occurs to me where he makes the German muse run a race with the British; and indeed, when one thinks what a picture it is, where the girls run one against the other, throwing about their legs, and kicking up the dust, one must assume that the good Klopstock did not really have before his eyes such pictures as he wrote, else he could not possibly have made such mistakes.—*Conversations of Goethe*, November 9, 1824.

Of these lines of Montgomery,—

> The soul aspiring pants its source to mount,
>
> As streams meander level to their fount,—

Macaulay observes:—

We take this to be, on the whole, the worst similitude in the world. In the first place, no stream meanders or can possibly meander level with the fount. In the next place, if streams did meander level with their founts, no two notions can be less like each other than that of meandering level and mounting upward.—Cited in Bartlett's *Familiar Quotations*.

It would be easy and it would be amusing to go on with examples of mixed figures and figures which are ineffective, but the point hardly needs further illustration.

Pushing a figure too far is a fault less common in these days than it has been at some periods of our literary history when fashions in writing were more ornate than at present. If a writer realizes what a simile means, he is not likely to fall into this error. It is when he introduces a figure for the sake of the figure, and not for the purpose of strengthening or making more clear what he is saying, that this fault occurs.

These lines of Cowper may serve as an example:

Man is a harp, whose chords elude the sight,
Each yielding harmony disposed aright;
The screws reversed (a task which, if He please,
God in a moment executes with ease),
Ten thousand thousand strings at once go loose,
Lost, till He tune them, all their power and use.

If this stopped with the second line, it might do well enough; but when the attention is forced to the consideration of the mechanical details of the harp, and the image of ten thousand thousand strings and a corresponding number of screws, and the notion applied to a man bereft of his wits, the idea becomes absurd, and whatever value the figure might have is entirely lost.

A clear realization of what he is doing will also prevent the writer from mingling figure and fact. "He was the guardian genius of Ireland, and had served with eloquence and credit in legislative halls," could hardly have been written by one who felt clearly the meaning and significance of the figure. To realize how a guardian genius would look in legislative halls would have brought him at once to his senses. It is always necessary to have sharply defined in the brain whatever one is saying, but this is especially true of any use of language which invites the reader to loose his grasp upon absolute, literal fact.

The difference between simile and metaphor is one which need not be pressed very sharply. It is to be observed that as writing becomes more excited or impassioned there is less need of insisting upon formalities; so that as the writer warms his readers, he may assume a likeness instead of explicitly stating it. At the beginning of a passage it may be better to say, "Napoleon swept like a tempest over Europe," whereas later, the reader having become interested in the theme, it is fitting to write, "Napoleon, the tempest which was sweeping over Europe." There is probably no better rule than for the writer to do that which at the moment seems to him most natural, and then in revision to see if it strikes him as it did when he wrote it.

Personification may be conveniently regarded as classed with simile and metaphor. It is somewhat out of fashion, but if it is used it is to be governed by the rules given above. One who realizes what he is saying in the phrase, "Hope told a flattering tale,"—who sees that he is representing Hope as a beautiful and seductive being,—is not likely to go on to add, "but this hope was founded upon a delusion," because he cannot conceive a young nymph or goddess as being founded upon anything. He will naturally and without effort carry out the figure, and say, "but she beguiled us;" or, "but all her flatteries were delusions." The truth is, that the mind will generally go in the right direction if it is given a fair chance. It is only when we hamper it with rules not understood, when we force it to go in paths which we suppose to be laid out by conventions, or when we endeavor to make it pace according to our vanity, that it goes astray. Be natural in the use of figures, and you will seldom be wrong.

VIII

Means and Effects Continued

Few means of literary effect are more subtle than Variety. It must pervade all parts of a composition, yet it is to be perceived only by its effects. Its absence is at once noted, and at once destroys the beauty and attractiveness of any work; yet to define Variety is as difficult as to tell how it is to be secured. Stevenson gives a rule as wise as it is hard to follow: "The one rule is to be infinitely various."

The need of variety in the use of words is evident. The fault of repetition is sufficiently obvious, yet it is very easily committed. The fact that a sentence has been written in a given form often makes that seem the only correct way of expression. No one but a thoroughly trained writer can be as sensitive to errors in his own work as to mistakes in the writings of others; and so it happens that unless one is very careful the same word may appear two or three times in a passage where synonyms would be better than the repetition. That richness in synonyms which is one of the finest characteristics of English does away with any necessary difficulty in attaining variety in diction. In writing, and yet more in revising, the value and force of synonymous terms cannot be too constantly kept in mind. A knowledge of these, with that cardinal virtue of writers, the dictionary-habit, should carry any student triumphantly past all dangers of monotony in words.

One caution should perhaps be added: Do not be afraid to repeat a word as often as is really necessary. I quoted in an earlier chapter a sentence from Lowell which illustrates what I mean:

The soil out of which such men as he are made is good to be born on, good to live on, good to die for and be buried in.

Or notice the repetition of "man" and of "department" in this from Macaulay:—

> A man possessed of splendid talents, which he often abused, and of sound judgment, the admonitions of which he often neglected; a man who succeeded only in an inferior department of his art, but who in that department succeeded preëminently.—*On John Dryden.*

Here the judicious repetition of the subject holds the whole closely together, and saves the attention of the reader from fatigue. It serves, also, to mark the distinction between the first half, which is a specification of the causes of failure, and the second half, which states the effects that followed from them. The recurrence of "department" adds to the emphasis in a way which may easily be appreciated by replacing it by a pronoun. Repetitions so cleverly used as this are of course not defects but beauties.

The variation of form is an art more cunning than that of the changing of the word. Look at this sentence from Stevenson, and notice how much is gained by the alteration of the construction:—

> How often and willingly do I not look in fancy on Tummel, or Manor, or the talking Ardle, or Dee swirling in its Lynn; on the bright burn of Kinnaird, or the golden burn that pours and sulks in the den behind Kingussie!—*Pastoral.*

To put "talking" before its noun and "swirling" after the substantive it modifies, to see to it that no two phrases shall have the same form, may seem small matters, and yet it is by devices of this sort that the skillful artificer of words gives to his style finish and charm.

The ability to command a variety of forms gives to the writer the power of repetition without seeming to repeat. Often it happens that it is well to re-say a thing, either for the sake of putting it in a light somewhat different from that of its first presentation, or to enforce it more strongly. This is especially true, it may be, of writing which is expository or argumentative, but the need of repetition of ideas is common to composition of all sorts. To vary the cadence of the sentence so that the ear shall never be wearied by monotony, cunningly to mix long and short paragraphs so that no single form constantly repeated shall tire the attention, is indeed a difficult art to acquire. No rule can be given for variety; the very idea of rule for variation involves a contradiction of terms, since it is the essence of variation to be irregular. The student must train his ear and his mind by reading the best authors; but the most that instruction can do is to call attention to this matter, and thus to afford a clue to what may be the real if unsuspected cause of a writer's dissatisfaction when his work appears vaguely dull and unattractive. Variety is closely connected with Elegance. The adaptation of the sentence structure to the thought, and yet more the subtler adaptation to the mood, are refinements of composition which it takes long to acquire; but with every advance toward a mastery of them the learner has come nearer to the secret of that consummate skill in fitting means to effects which is the soul of the highest style. Each must do it for himself; for the secret of variety cannot be told farther than it is revealed in the words of Stevenson, with which we began: "The one rule is to be infinitely various."

Upon variety depends largely that delightful and elusive quality which we call Euphony. No writer or reader can be long insensible to that music of words which is as intangibly tangible in prose as in poetry,—different in the one from the other, but as real and truly a source of delight in speech as in song, in prose as in verse. It is true that what is written is not necessarily read aloud. It is written in silence, and untrained writers fail to realize that although it be read in silence, the eye is the ear of the mind, and all melody or lack of melody will be subtilely felt in the soundless perusal. All that has been said of variety applies as well to this quality; and, indeed, it is perhaps hardly necessary to give two names where the two things are so closely interwoven.

Intangible as this quality may seem, it is yet one of the most striking in literature. Take this sentence from Walt Whitman, and see if it is possible for any reader not to be offended by its close:—

Nor shades of Virgil, nor myriad memories, poems, old associations, magnetize and hold on to her.

Or suppose one said:—

If for the city of Athens nature did much, it is not to be denied that art did a great deal more.

The ear is dull which does not perceive the difference between this and the sentence as Newman wrote it:—

If nature did much for Athens, it is undeniable that art did much more.

Examples might be multiplied indefinitely, but it is better that the student find them for himself. Sensitiveness to euphony and the practical acquirement of a euphonious style are greatly aided by the habit of reading aloud the works of men who are masters, and it is well to test in the same way whatever is written. The ear is more readily trained by the voice than by any other means. It is possible to suppose that what we have written must sound well as a matter of course; but if we read or hear it read aloud, and find that it does not please the ear, only one stupid with self-conceit will leave it unaltered. A melodious diction is apt to be made up more largely of short words than of long ones, and of words easily pronounced than of those trying to the tongue; yet it is no more possible to achieve a euphonious style simply by using words short and easily pronounced than it is to make a beautiful brook by digging a channel which shall be entirely straight and free from obstructions, or to build a beautiful temple by collecting exquisite marbles. Construction is more than material.

One of the means by which it was formerly the fashion to strive after pleasing sound in diction was the use of alliteration. This device is somewhat in disrepute in these days, because it has been so notoriously abused. The sensational novelist could no more do without alliteration than without the historical present tense. The patent medicines are alliteratively labeled; comic operas and pseudo-Queen Anne cottages at little watering-places have been baptized with titles with reduplicated initials, until the writer who indulges in alliteration feels something as does the professor who sees his title blazoned on the shingle of the barber and the boot-black.

Yet this pleasant device cannot be spared. There is in our blood some trace of the fondness for it which made it serve the old bards instead of rhyme. It must be employed more cunningly than of old, and as it were slipped into the literary web surreptitiously. Here are instances:—

A man is a bundle of *relations*, a knot of *roots*, whose *flower* and *fruitage* is the world.—Emerson: *History*.

In making education not only *common* to all, but in some sense *compulsory* on all.—Lowell: *New England Two Centuries Ago*.

All the beautiful *sentiments* in the *world weigh* less than a *single* lovely action.—*Id.: Rousseau and the Sentimentalists*.

Here there is little more than the repetition of the initial of a prominent word, marked by the same place in successive cadences. Often alliteration in modern prose of the best sort is carried much farther. Here are a couple of examples from Stevenson:—

I know a child of Suffolk whose fancy still *lingers* about the *lilied lowland* waters of that shire.—*Pastoral*.

A task in *recitation* that *really* merited *reward*.—*The Manse*.

Of course I am speaking only of prose. The diction of poetry is governed by different laws, and the reduplication of sound is a recognized and not infrequent ornament of verse used to a degree which would not be tolerated in prose. In the latter it is important that alliteration shall appear to be rather the consequence of the subject than an extraneous ornament. Once a writer introduces into prose a word which is evidently or even apparently chosen for its initial, he has given the reader a suspicion of artificiality which is fatal to the best effect.

Alliteration is, however, more readily allowed in epigram and antithesis than in plain, straightforward passages. The writer is permitted some especial graces of ornament when he attempts either of these, as a child may without remark wear its best raiment to a party when its companions would jeer at such display at school. "Forms are the food of faith," writes Newman. "All mankind love a lover," Emerson says. These epigrams are openly alliterative. No less so is the well-known antithesis of Macaulay, "The Puritans hated bear-baiting, not because it gave pain to the bear, but because it gave pleasure to the spectator."

The epigram has the great advantage of recalling the proverb; and proverbs will ever be dear to the heart of man as the purses in which have been preserved the homely wisdom of the world. It is perhaps in part because of its family likeness to the proverb that it seems not unfitting for the epigram to balance word against word in a way which would seem artificial in any other form of expression.

The mention of epigram and antithesis reminds us that it is well to speak briefly of both.

Antithesis is the setting formally against each other of contrasting thoughts. I might make an example if I wrote: Epigram is a sword with one edge; but antithesis is a blade with two. I should at the same time be expressing to some extent the characteristics of these verbal forms. Antithesis defines by differences; epigram emphasizes a single idea. One confesses its artificiality by its balanced structure; the other endeavors to hide it under an appearance of lucky spontaneity. Antithesis is obviously deliberate; epigram must have an air of quickness, as if it were the birth of the moment. The former belonged to the elaborate style of a more ceremonious age; the latter has been cultivated in the prose of our own time until it has almost become a vice.

The above paragraph, which is largely antithetical, shows the limitation of this form. It is not possible long to continue this sort of writing without wearying the reader with a sense of artificiality. Such pleasure as the present age is willing to take in undisguised effort in prose is largely confined to the epigram.

An epigram is a notion rounded like a snowball f or throwing. Looked at in another way, it is a thought packed for quick transportation. It is wit or wisdom given wings; or, if it be neither, it is at least an idea with its loins girt for running. Sometimes it is a base or worthless reflection set in terse phrase, like a fly in amber; or a cruel insinuation wounding like a wasp with envenomed sting. At its best it is a jewel of price; at its worst it is a drop of subtle poison.

Here, somewhat at the risk of confusing by a variety of images, I have tried to write a short paragraph which is practically all in the form of epigrams. It is in turn evident that although less obviously artificial than antithesis, epigrams are apt to lack spontaneity, no matter how much they strive for it. It is difficult to incorporate them into ordinary prose so that they shall seem really to be an integral part of it. An epigram is apt to be like a shell, so complete and individual in itself that it is hard to make it appear to be a part of any other whole. Skillfully handled, the epigram gives crispness and vigor to a style, but by so much the more as it is effective if successful it is damaging if it fails. It is to be remembered, too, that the habit of striving for any especial verbal form is a dangerously fascinating one. It is easy to fall into the way of making phrases for their own sake, instead of for the purpose of expressing what one has to say. An epigram is valuable and commendable only in so far as it serves the purpose for which it is contrived. The Greeks used the word originally to signify a verse inscribed on a tomb, and not a few modern epigrams are the epitaphs of thoughts killed in making them.

We are accustomed to-day to employ the word for any concise and terse expression of thought, and to call that style epigrammatic which is distinguished by conciseness and by brief and pregnant sentences. Broadly speaking, so long as the writer keeps in mind that the epigram is to aid expression, and that intention is never to be sacrificed to form, the more of these qualities his style has the better. He must remember, moreover, that the ear must be relieved by sentences of varied length. The successful epigram is almost always brief, and it must contain an element of novelty. One of its chief claims to attention is that it puts its thought in a form which excites surprise. It is like the German bonbon, which parts with a startling snap and discloses a gift within.

The more it has the air of being the result of an instantaneous, happy inspiration, the more effective is it. An epigram must seem at least to be like the poet, born and not made.

This matter of novelty concerns more than epigram. Words and phrases become worn as surely as coins which have long passed from hand to hand. Epithets which have been constantly repeated lose the force of their original intent and fail to produce their first effect. The masters of style do not hesitate now and then to coin new words with which to serve themselves in the attempt to produce pungent effects which old terms no longer yield. Carlyle is an extreme example of this, and a list of the extraordinary novelties which he boldly made for his own use would fill pages. He exposed himself to the danger of losing the impression which he produced as soon as the words invented lost their first novelty, and no doubt something of the diminution of the influence of Carlyle which we have lived to see is due to this very cause. The ordinary writer is not allowed thus to serve his need by invention. He must be content to take words already in use, and must display his ingenuity by contriving so to employ them that from old terms he brings freshness of effect.

The novelty which is within the reach of all is that of originality. It seems at first startling to speak of originality as within common reach when we take up every day books wherein the writers show so absolute a lack of all originality that they shake one's very belief in original sin. Yet remember what Flaubert said to De Maupassant: "The smallest thing has in it something unknown. Discover it…. That is the way to become original." Life can never appear the same to any two human beings, because no two look at it with the same eyes or with the same mind. The original writer is he who sets down his own thoughts, who shows to others what is exactly in his own brain and heart. It is not within the power of every author thus to create profoundly fresh and inspiring works; but it is within the reach of all to say something which shall be at once new and individual and vital.

What is called individuality is the result of this frank and sincere speaking of the thought which comes to the writer and as it comes to the writer. It is needful to be on one's guard lest sometimes instead of being guided by sincerity and natural honesty one fall into the trick of using particular forms of diction or construction. We are all exposed to the danger of imitating ourselves. Having once written a thing which by its honesty and frankness was impressive, there is a temptation to go on repeating the same thing or to try to do something which shall seem like it. In this way arise what are known as mannerisms. The difference between individuality and mannerism is that between sincerity and egotism; between personality and affectation. Individuality in style is an honest embodying of that which makes the writer different from any other man alive; mannerism is the sham—if unconscious—effort to appear different. Be truthfully exact in saying nothing but what is really felt, and individuality is as sure as mannerism is impossible.

Read what Lowell says of Chaucer:—

Chaucer seems to me to have been one of the most purely original of poets.... He is original not in the sense that he thinks and says what nobody ever thought or said before, and what nobody can ever think and say again, but because he is always natural; because, if not absolutely new, he is always delightfully fresh; because he sets before us the world as it honestly appeared to Geoffrey Chaucer, and not a world as it seemed proper to certain people that it ought to appear.

There you have the whole of it. He who is least concerned about being original, and most engrossed in expressing precisely the thought and the feeling which have come to him, is in the end the writer who is most vitally and perennially fresh. Think new thoughts always if you can; but above all do not put a thought upon paper unless you so honestly and sincerely think it that it does not occur to you to consider whether anybody else has or has not said this thing before.

IX

Classification

Thus far we have spoken of the general principles of composition, and of qualities which are common to all attempts to express thought by written language. There are so many ways, however, in which composition may be employed, that for further consideration it is convenient to divide it into classes. We have come to the place where it is well to serve ourselves with some division of the sorts of writing, just as we before found it well to serve ourselves by the separation of general principles.

Classification is necessary in any study, not only for convenience in handling, but for clearness of conception. If ideas are arranged systematically, they not only are remembered more easily, but their mutual relations are discovered, and their relative values more accurately estimated. It is of importance, however, to recognize that in all investigations classification is not an end, but a means. He who classifies clears the way for future work, either of his own or of others, but he does not necessarily reach anything permanent or effective in itself. The student of botany may analyze and tabulate all the plants in the land; but if he has not reached out toward general truths and fundamental principles, it cannot be said that he has learned much. He has amused himself, perhaps has had a good deal of healthful out-of-door life, and a certain amount of mental gymnastics,—but that is the whole of it. Classification, and especially classification which is not original, is not the attainment of knowledge in any high sense.

I pause to comment upon this at more length than the connection warrants, strictly speaking, because the subject is one of so great general importance. Everywhere in his studies the learner finds classification set up as a ladder by means of which he may climb to knowledge. Most students fall to counting the rungs of the ladder, to measuring the spaces between them, to informing themselves carefully who made it. Unless in the waste of time there is no harm in this, if, after all, the ladder be really used, and if the learner be clear-headed enough to realize that all this is of no more than relative value. Classification is the means by which the mind is able to master a subject, but it is not the subject itself. To classify originally it is necessary to understand the relations of things, and the investigators by whom classes are defined must of course be thoroughly well informed in regard to the facts upon which arrangement is based. The ordinary student is constantly in danger of accepting the formal schedule instead of the truths which it represents; of filling his mind with nomenclature instead of principles; of being, in a word, satisfied with system in place of knowledge.

All essential and ultimate knowledge is natural, and all classification is artificial. Classification is founded upon natural facts, but it is an enumeration rather than an elucidation. It arranges; it does not explain.

Understand that I do not undervalue classification. The student can no more advance without it than he could climb to a roof without a ladder. I merely wish to impress upon you the fact that in all work—and perhaps especially in scientific work—it is of the highest importance to keep steadily in mind that it is not the ladder but the ascent which is of consequence; that the aim is not the schedule but the secrets of wisdom to which it helps us.

Thus it is that it is not for any value in the distinction itself, but solely as an expedient for our convenience in acquiring knowledge which is of worth, that we divide the sorts of composition. We classify, as in microscopy it is necessary to make sections for ease of examination. Do not fail to classify; but do not fail also to remember that nomenclature is not knowledge, that classification is not wisdom.

It is hardly necessary to remark how varied are the effects which writers may endeavor to produce. One is intent simply upon giving a clear and prosaic account of some matter; making a straightforward appeal to the understanding, and not troubling himself to go beyond this. A second is bent upon conveying to his readers some emotion, overpowering or delicate, painful or joyous, as the case may be. A third aims only to amuse; a fourth is determined to convince, to persuade, or to overcome; and so on through the long list of objects which are conceivable as coming within the scope of the writer's range of intention.

Obviously, the treatment must be varied as the effect sought alters, and we divide compositions into classes by their most strongly marked characteristics. Different authorities have varied the number of divisions, and I have not felt bound to follow any of them. It seems to me well to assume that the kinds of composition are Exposition, Argument, Description, and Narration; and to take up their examination in this order.

From the classification commonly received this differs in a change of order and in the omission of Persuasion. Some writers, indeed, include here both Criticism and Translation; but Criticism is really a species of exposition, while Translation is whatever sort of composition its original may happen to be. That Persuasion should so long have been retained in the list is curious, although not so strange as might appear from the name. Persuasion, in the strict sense of the term, is of course not a kind of composition, but a quality of style. An argument, an exposition, a narrative, must alike be persuasive to succeed in winning the reader. Indeed, persuasion is a quality essential to all art. In the sense of being that which leads others to submit their personality to the artist, it is necessary to painter, musician, sculptor, and architect, no less than to writer. As used to designatea department of composition, Persuasion has been that which addresses, which appeals to the passions directly.[3] The term is not a happy one, since it would seem that the vocative—the mood of

---

3   Professor Hill's definition of Persuasion seems to me to make it an argument which appeals to selfish prejudices or emotions.

address—might include denunciation, or invective, or praise, as well as persuasion. The obvious explanation of the use of such a division of composition seems to be that it was made to provide a place of dignity for oratory. In the days of our forefathers the art of eloquence held a high station, such as it is not likely to occupy soon again; and it was evidently felt that there should be a separate department for it in formal rhetoric. Persuasion as a division of composition seems to have been provided for oratory, much as a sinecure is established for a court favorite; but since platform eloquence has fallen somewhat into obscurity, it has been realized that Exposition and Argument cover the whole ground. If such a division were to exist still, it would be better to call it Oratory and be done with it; but if there were to be a fifth kind of composition, there is more ground for trespassing on the domain of Narrative and naming it Dramatization.

As a reason for departing from the time-honored custom of putting Description and Narrative before Exposition and Argument, I might perhaps content myself with saying that it is being found by instructors in whose judgment I have the highest confidence that the new order is the better. This is in part due to the fact that inexperienced writers naturally suppose that they can describe and narrate without having had especial training, and it is less difficult to detach them from bad habits of composition, if they begin with a sort of writing in which they have not contracted faults already. To put pupils in advanced composition first upon Description and Narration is apt to be to expose them to the danger of repeating whatever bad literary habits they may have, since it is in these forms of production that they are most likely to have contracted them. Another point of importance is that Description and Narration are so much more attractive and easily emotional than Exposition and Argument. I have already said that technique can be readily mastered only in an unemotional way. The great performers upon musical instruments have almost always been those who were trained technically while they were still so young or so undeveloped that the emotional capabilities of their nature were not matured. There is great danger in allowing the emotions to be aroused while training which is merely technical is going on. Awaken in the pupil all interest in technical perfection which is possible; to excite his emotional interest in subject or sentiment is dangerous, and obstructs his progress in the cultivation of skill in form and technique. Technical facility is gained by work not in itself inspiring, but done with the most patient exactness for the sake of the power it gives.

Assuming, then, that it is convenient to consider composition as being divided into the four sorts named, and that there are sufficient reasons for taking them in the order given, we find it necessary next to define. Making broad definitions, and leaving finer distinctions to be considered later, we may say:—

Exposition is a statement, an explanation, or a setting forth.

Argument is the endeavor to establish the truth or falsity of an idea or a proposition.

Description is the endeavor to present a picture.

Narration is a record of events.

If a traveler, for instance, should write of the Acropolis at Athens, he might treat the subject in any one of several ways. If he discuss its architectural character, its beauty, and the æsthetic feelings of delight which this awakens, if he explain its use, or make statements of any sort about it, he is making an Exposition; if he endeavor to establish the truth or untruth of especial views of its use, of theories of its age, or of any matters subject to controversy, he passes into Argument; if he by words strives to call up in the mind of the reader a picture of that glorious ruin, he is describing it; while, if he tell the story of the temple, he is evidently dealing in Narrative.

It is hardly necessary to say that these varieties of composition melt into one another. In a work of any extent, it is generally probable that all of them will be employed. As an engraver, cutting his block of box-wood, uses first one tool and then another, according to the line demanded by the picture, striving to bring out the effect which the artist desires, so the skilled writer takes up one variety of composition after another, employs now this and now that. It is the old question of adapting the method to the end sought, the effort to the effect desired. In almost any book there will be found Exposition, Argument, Description, and Narrative, as in a single rose are sepals, petals, stamens, and pistils. We study these separately, but always the art of writing is one as the rose is one.

X

Exposition

Doubtless you all remember the amazement of the "Bourgeois Gentilhomme" of Molière when he suddenly discovered that he had been speaking prose all his life without suspecting it. We may be in the same situation when it first becomes clear to us that without being aware of it we have been making expositions from the time we began first to speak. The statements, the explanations, the opinions which we give by hundreds every day are simply expositions in little. What we have to do now is merely to discover if possible what are the principles which will make the same sort of thing effective when it is carried further than in common speech, and is put in written instead of in spoken words.

To expound is to set forth the nature, the significance, the characteristics, and the bearing of an idea or a group of ideas. Exposition therefore differs from Description in that it deals directly with the meaning or intent of its subject instead of with its appearance. A good deal which we are accustomed inexactly to call description is really exposition. Suppose that your small boy wishes to know how an engine works, and should say: "Please describe the steam-engine to me." If you insist upon taking his words literally—and are willing to run the risk of his indignation at being willfully misunderstood,—you will to the best of your ability picture to him this familiarly wonderful machine. If you explain it to him, you are not describing but expounding it; you are not making a Description but an Exposition, in so far as these words are applied in our present sense. The exact boundary lines of Exposition—or, for that matter, of any sort of composition—it is impossible to draw sharply. Not everything which claims to explain really makes clear, any more than all which wears the air of virtue shall escape scorching in "the everlasting bonfire." One thing merges into another, and in the end all composition, as has been said and repeated already, is an indivisible whole.

The inexactness with which all terms of classification are used and must be used in literature is illustrated by the extension of the word "essay," under which are grouped so many sorts of expositions. It has become the custom to apply this name to almost any brief monograph of leisurely or reflective character. The critical papers of Hazlitt, the historical orgies of Macaulay, the humorous confidences of Charles Lamb, and the argumentative tracts of Newman on theology or of Ruskin upon social questions, are all loosely classed together as essays. In contemporary writings, the suggestive mediæval studies of Vernon Lee, papers by Walter Pater from which the life has been exquisitely elaborated, the intimate revelations of nature by Richard Jefferies or John Burroughs, the delightful word-sonatas of Stevenson, and the criticisms of Leslie Stephen, fine and scholarly, are all given the same convenient name. The term "essay" is not unlike that useful contrivance known to travelers as a "hold-all," into which may be huddled whatever there is not room for in more dignified receptacles. Fortunately the harm done is too small to matter. If a thing is good it is of no great consequence what we call it.

In an age like this, when the magazine flourishes and newspapers are thick strewn like sodden leaves in a November storm, the exposition is naturally one of the most common and one of the most practically useful of all forms of composition. The modern endeavor to make all men understand everything of course renders necessary an enormous amount of expository writing; so that the press turns out daily and hourly an innumerable number of small essays upon all imaginable topics. We live in an expository era. The scientific spirit demands that all knowledge shall be set forth, often to the discouragement of more imaginative forms of composition. This sort of work is certainly the one for which there is to-day the most constant and urgent call. The utilitarian would get along pretty much to his own satisfaction if no other form of writing than Exposition had been invented; and this is a utilitarian age.

Of all the qualities which we have hitherto considered, the one most likely to tell in Exposition is Clearness. In practical work the essential thing here is to make accurately intelligible the meaning which the writer would convey. In all more delicate matters this is impossible without recourse to the higher arts of literary technique; but in general all grace of style, all persuasiveness of presentation, all elegance of proportion and of manner, are subordinated to this primary necessity of lucidity. If one is striving to produce permanent literature these must not be neglected; but as far as common, practical, workaday prose is concerned, everything else is considered as of less importance than the conveying to the reader with sharpness the exact significance of what the writer is endeavoring to phrase.

Two things may be briefly remarked in passing: First, that this characteristic need of clear-cut accuracy makes especially appropriate the taking up of Exposition at the start; and second, that this sort of composition is of great help in intellectual growth. It is not that the other forms of expression do not call for accuracy. There is as much need for exactness in the imparting of fine shades of emotion suggested by a description or by a narrative as in the statement of an opinion. It is more easy, however, for the student to grasp the more tangible matter than the more subtile. He more readily appreciates the process of direct expression than that of delicate implication. It is true that Exposition in its higher forms deals with thought and emotion; but even there it handles them rather in a direct than in an indirect manner, rather by statement than by suggestion.

It is not difficult to see how the practice of this sort of composition is an aid to intellectual progress. Indeed, education is after all largely the phrasing for ourselves a statement of the truths of life and of the world about us. This sort of writing forces the learner to think sharply and clearly, to realize his thoughts. Exposition leads the student really to think instead of contenting himself with that mental muddlement in which the mind goes around and around, playfully like a kitten chasing its tail or earnestly after the fashion of a squirrel in his wheel, but getting ahead in neither case.

The two qualities which are, after clearness, most valuable in this species of writing are unity of the whole work and progression. The nature of Unity has already been sufficiently commented upon, but it is worth while to speak of a mechanical device by which much can be done to secure it. This is the making of a plan of an exposition before writing it. I have seldom found a student who willingly wrote out a skeleton of an exercise, and authors are hardly less reluctant to bother to put upon paper the plan of an essay. I am aware from my own experience how many excuses for not doing this necessary piece of drudgery may be invented by the evasive mind. It is of course a bore, when the head is full of a theme, to be obliged to stop and in a cold-blooded manner construct the framework of the essay which we are eager to dash off at full speed. Yet in the end it is a saving of time. It is better to do this in the first place than to have to pull the work to pieces afterward. When the mind is alert and excited, make notes, phrase the vital portions of the essay, set down the significant thoughts which come to you; but before attempting to write the completed whole have all these notes, these images, these phrases, arranged with reference to a plan, a schedule of the entire composition. This may be slight, but it should be essentially complete in the sense that it covers the whole ground. I believe it to be practically impossible for any writer to secure unity in a work of any extent without making a preliminary plan of some kind; and only men of rare gifts and much experience can safely carry this in the head. It is certainly true that the inexperienced writer should not trust himself to attempt any composition more than a page or two in length without actually writing out a skeleton beforehand.

As a matter of practical work, a young writer who is attempting an exposition should begin by thinking out his subject and putting his thoughts on paper. He should strive to phrase them well when he makes his first memoranda, for thoughts are like metal, much more malleable when they are hot. Often an ugly phrase which could without much trouble have been improved when it was making becomes stubbornly intractable after it has been for a time on paper. It is convenient to have these notes on slips of paper, since it is thus easy to arrange and to rearrange them. It is also of importance to consider how a subject will appear to a reader whose views are opposed to those of the writer. Think up all possible objections that might be made to the ideas expressed. Turn the subject over, and examine the wrong side; this is the best way to judge of the strength and the smoothness of the seams by which the parts are joined to make a whole.

The next step is to arrange the thoughts noted down. Make a plan of the essay with reference to its logical continuity. Look at the framework as a single thing. Remember that it is upon the completeness and sufficiency of this that the finished work must depend for its unity and its effect as a whole. To this scheme fit your notes. Do not trouble as yet about ornament or finish unless pregnant illustration or happy phrase suggest itself unsought. You cannot afford to go seeking these graces until the more substantial portions of your work are practically complete. Write slowly or swiftly according to your temperament,—but whatever your temperament do not suppose that good work is to be done otherwise than systematically and thoroughly.

Once the form is complete, the more you finish and polish the better. It is true that it is possible to polish the life out of a composition; but this is a danger much farther along the road than I should presume to act as a guide. I do not suppose that any author liable to spoil his work from over-finish is likely to trouble himself about what I may say on the subject; and certainly this fault lies so far ahead of most of us that we need not from fear of it stay our hand.

When the essay is planned and written and polished, and if possible laid aside and taken out and polished over again,—why, then, I am tempted to say, the wisest rule is that given by Edward Lear for the making of "Crumbobblious Cutlets:" "Procure some strips of beef, and having cut them into the smallest possible slices, proceed to cut them still smaller,—eight or perhaps nine times." When you have made the work as good as you can make it, proceed to make it better still,—eight or perhaps nine times!

It is not impossible that it may occur to you that this sounds a good deal like hard work. I said to you in the beginning that to succeed in writing is a laborious task. It is a task infinitely interesting, and it is this which makes it endurable. The fine arts are possible only because men do not spare labor even if what is done must be wrought in the sweat of the brow and with the blood of the heart; art lives because the artist works from love, and does not count the cost. Unless the worker is willing thus to labor at literature, he will do well to leave it alone. If his heart is not in it he will in the end but waste good paper and ink which might have served better workmen for better uses.

Keeping still to practical details, we may note that it is well to accustom the mind to measure compositions by the number of words. This is the professional method, and it is the only way of coming at a fairly accurate idea of the size of a work and the proportionate length of its parts. It is not difficult to get into the mind a standard in the number of words one usually writes on a page. Once this is done, the rest is easy. The page becomes a personal measure of extent, and by it one without difficulty estimates the bulk of the whole or any part of a manuscript. Whoever has dealings with periodicals or with publishers is sure to come to this question of the number of words sooner or later, and it is well to learn it early.

One of the cleverest of American playwrights told me that he had made a careful study of the dramas of the modern French authors to see how many words they use to produce an effect. So many words he found to be the average for a love scene, so many in this situation and so many in that. It was not that he endeavored to follow exactly these rules; but he was thus getting at the secrets of construction. This was a practical method of judging proportions. The incident is worth mention not only as an illustration of the way in which words are used as a measure in literature, but also as showing how tirelessly and with what minute care the professional worker is willing to labor.

One of the first practical uses to which the student is called to apply this measure of the number of words is that of estimating proportion. The space given to any division of a subject, the number of words in which it is embodied, largely determines its relation to the whole. It is somewhat difficult to illustrate this point, but by way of indicating the sort of analysis which it is well for the student now and then to make of essays which he finds especially effective, I must give an example. I have taken Macaulay's essay of Machiavelli, and made a summary of it with a view of showing the proportionate length at which this clever author writes of the different points upon which he touches. In this paper he is setting forth his view of the character of that dazzlingly clever Italian whose family name has furnished the language with an epithet for whatever is most trickily cunning, while by an absurd paradox his Christian name is held to have given us an affectionate pseudonym for the devil,—"Old Nick." The whole monograph is something in the nature of a special plea, and without great violation of propriety might be smuggled under Argument. It is an attempt to show that the characteristics in the writings of Machiavelli which have made his name a hissing and a byword belong rather to the time than to the man.

After a brief introduction follows a statement of the disrepute in which Machiavelli has been held. This is intentionally made strong to the verge of absurdity, and to it is added a brief acknowledgment that "The Prince," Machiavelli's famous and infamous book, is indeed shocking. This requires about three hundred and fifty words.

Assuming the attitude which he wishes the reader to take, that of a puzzled seeker for truth, Macaulay states several theories which might account for the moral obliquity of the Italian, yet points out that his personal career was elevated, patriotic, and just; and that there is in "The Prince" much good as well as much evil. He also calls attention to the fact that at the time the book was written it apparently shocked nobody. To this are given about eight hundred words.

This leads directly to the conclusion which is the key-note of the whole essay:—

It is, therefore, in the state of moral feeling among the Italians of those times that we must seek for the real explanation of what seems most mysterious in the life of this remarkable man.

This proposition being the one which it is the aim of the essay to establish, nearly seventy-five hundred words, almost half of the whole, are given to tracing the growth of the peculiar conditions of moral sentiment which obtained in Italy in the time when Machiavelli wrote. The subject is led on toward the next point in this way:—

Every age and every nation has certain characteristic vices.... Posterity, ... finding the delinquents too numerous to be all punished, ... selects some of them at hazard to bear the whole penalty.... In the present case the lot has fallen on Machiavelli; a man whose public conduct was upright and honorable.

The essayist then turns from the man to his work, pointing out the merits of his novels, comedies, and letters. About twenty-three hundred words are given to this,—rather more than an eighth of the paper. Some eighteen hundred follow on his public services. His struggles to establish a regular army are emphasized, both because here he appears to the best advantage, and because this line of thought is artfully made to lead up to and to suggest the view of "The Prince" which is put forward immediately after: the view that the book was really designed to forward the substitution of a regular army for the mercenary troops which had demoralized all Italy. The proportion is here admirably judged. Enough space is given to the matter to make the point seem one of dignity and weight, yet not so much as to let it appear as if the author were insisting upon it too much. The economy of effect is observed throughout; enough is always done, but never too much.

We have now, roughly speaking, thirteen thousand out of the not much over sixteen thousand words in the essay; and the author has practically done his work. He has pretty well developed his theory, and the remainder of the monograph is given to making it more clear and to enforcing it. To the personal merit of Machiavelli is devoted about a quarter of the entire essay; to the immorality of the age and its influence upon him, nearly one half; to the admirable way in which he played his part in public life, nearly an eighth. To the hatred and abhorrence of Machiavelli which the essayist desires to overcome, he gives directly but three or four hundred words in the whole sixteen thousand. Proportion so careful and so effective as this can only be the result of studied and accurate design.

A word of caution may not be amiss. Proportion is to be determined not by the interest of the writer or by his ease in writing upon particular points, but by the relation of the parts to the whole. The reason for saying this is that almost any author is liable to be led away by the facility with which it is possible for him to enlarge upon certain points. An opportunity presents itself for the introduction of a charming episode; there is a temptation to develop a thought, a sentiment, a seductively favorite theory; and the result of yielding to this is apt to be a violation of unity. What the old-fashioned writers—as if confession were an excuse—were accustomed to confess by saying, "But this is a digression," hopelessly injured the effect of a composition as a whole. Only the clever and cunning artificer of style can introduce digressions without marring the fair proportions of the complete work.

Proportion, here as elsewhere, is emotional as well as mechanical. One must bear in mind the fact that a few emphatic words are of more account than many mild and commonplace ones. Consider not only the space given to particular portions of a work, but the stress laid upon them.

And here it is well to consider a feature of human frailty. Such is man's weakness that blame always counts for more than praise. If I were to say to you that looked at from a purely literary standpoint "The Heavenly Twins" is morbid and unhealthy rubbish; that "Trilby" is a pleasant transient excitement; but that "The Return of the Native" seems to me the most notable English novel since Thackeray— you would have no difficulty in remembering that I condemned "The Heavenly Twins;" you would have a fairly clear idea that I had been less enthusiastic than is the general public about "Trilby;" and you would perhaps recall vaguely that there was something else—really it is astonishing how quickly a name slips from the memory!—which I praised.[4] The point is one to be remembered when one is dealing with delicate shades of emphasis.

As I have more than once used Carlyle in warning, it is no more than fair to mention him here as one of the masters of emotional emphasis. He had an instinct for the proportion of stress, and used it with the greatest success. It is an excellent lesson in the study of this quality to analyze the cumulative and unified effect of the stronger chapters of the "French Revolution."

I have spoken of progression as being one of the important matters to be considered in connection with Exposition. Perhaps a better name for what I mean would be continuity. It is necessary to arrange ideas in a logical order which is not only unbroken, but which is perfectly obvious. It is not enough that the author is aware how one thought logically follows another; he must make it evident to all who read. He must remember that so long as the connection of ideas is clear and inevitable the reader is led on unconsciously; while every pause which the reader is forced to make to see how one statement follows from another leaves him less fully in the author's control. So great a thinker and so great a writer as Emerson materially lessened the circle of his readers by a lack of this very quality. The ordinary student often finds it hard to supply the thoughts which make the sequence of ideas complete. Emerson stalks like a giant from mountain peak of thought to mountain peak, while the reader is often sorely puzzled to know how to cross the deep gullies between. Emerson was a genius, and prophesied so gloriously on his mountain-tops, that we struggle forward after him despite all difficulties. Those who are not

---

4 A droll incident happened in connection with this illustration when these lectures were first delivered. As the audience left the hall one lady said to another, a stranger: "I beg your pardon, but could you tell me the name of the third book that was given,—the one that the lecturer said we should forget?" This was of course conclusive of nothing, but it was amusingly to the point.

geniuses cannot hope that readers will follow their lead unless the road is shown and the chasms bridged.

One may go farther than this in insisting upon the need of continuousness in literature. The present age is impatient of being called upon to take trouble in apprehension, so that it is necessary to use every art—whether of connectives, of arrangement of thought, of sequence of ideas or incidents—to make more inevitably evident the connection of parts. Indeed, this must be not only plain but easy and attractive. To blaze out a path through the woods avails in pioneer life and in the beginnings of literature; but when civilization has advanced, the way must be graded until it is comfortable to the foot accustomed to smooth pavements and velvet carpets. Sequence in expository writing should usually be so complete that the reader goes forward so glidingly that the mere progress itself shall be a pleasure.

XI

Exposition Continued

In expository writing—and indeed the rule might safely be applied to all composition—it is wise to proceed from the near to the remote; from cause to effect; from the physical to the mental; from the clear to the obscure; and from that which is generally allowed to that which is doubtful or disputed.

It is well to proceed from the near to the remote. We do not say "All the way from London to here," but "All the way from here to London." The exception would be when the point of view is that of one in London, since then that city would be the near, and "here" the remote. "Near" in this connection is always near to the point of view. We say, "What we do will be talked of all the way from here to London." We say also, "When Tom came home from England last year, he was ill all the way from London to here." We begin with that which the mind accepts most readily. The principle is the same which we have already found to underlie the use of figurative language. There the unknown is made clear by comparison with the known; and it is well to lead the mind from what is near, physically or mentally, to what is remote. Take this example from Stevenson:—

> It is difficult to see why the fellow does a thing so nameless and yet so formidable to look at, unless on the theory that he likes it. I suspect that is why; and I suspect it is at least ten per cent. of why Lord Beaconsfield and Mr. Gladstone have debated so much in the House of Commons, and why Burnaby rode to Khiva the other day, and why the Admirals courted war like a mistress.—*The English Admirals.*

This was published in England, and at a time when the speeches of Lord Beaconsfield and Mr. Gladstone were matters of every-day comment in the newspaper; the ride to Khiva was famous, but not so near in place or in realization, while the bravery of the English Admirals was part of history stretching back for centuries.

Here is illustration from Lowell:—

J. H., one of those choice poets who will not tarnish their bright fancies by publication, always insists on a snowstorm as essential to the true atmosphere of whist. Mrs. Battles, in her famous rule for the game, implies winter, and doubtless would have added tempest, if it could be had for the asking. For a good, solid read also, into the small hours, there is nothing like that sense of safety against having your evening laid waste, which Euroclydon brings, as he bellows down the chimney.—*A Good Word for Winter.*

Here we are given the pleasant saying of a neighbor, such as any of us might have heard; we go on to Mrs. Battles, dear to every reader of Elia; and from that to Euroclydon, the wind which put the apostle in danger of his life.

The same principle of course holds good in dealing wholly with ideas. Speaking of Leonardo da Vinci, Walter Pater writes:—

He brooded over the hidden virtues of plants and crystals, the lines traced by the stars as they moved in the sky, over the correspondences which exist between the different orders of living things, through which, to eyes opened, they interpret each other; and for years he seemed to those about him as one listening to a voice silent for other men.

From the idea of the virtues of plants and crystals, things which one might hold in the hand, the mind is led to the stars, far yet visible; while only after this is introduced the mysterious and intangible bond which has been conceived of as existing between all living things. Last of all is the suggestion of that thing still more remote, the silent voice heard only by the artist of all men who walked the earth.

I read in a scientific book the other day, in the description of a proposed machine, "On account of difficulty in handling and great weight, this is unsuitable." Here the effect is put before the cause, and the result is a loss of smoothness in progression. The point of view is that of a scientist who knows all about the machine, and he should have written: "great weight and consequent difficulty of handling." If the point of view were that of an investigator, the phrase might perhaps properly be, "difficulty in handling consequent upon the great weight," because the investigator would discover first the difficulty and then reflect upon the cause. This may seem a little like hair splitting, but no principle can be too closely examined, and for the student there is no such thing as being too careful in the study of means and effects.

We shall have occasion to speak of this matter again, particularly in its application to description. Here it is enough to add that the simplest course is to follow in writing the order which seems most natural; and then in revision to apply the rule given at the beginning of this chapter.

The order which seems most natural will generally be that in which the thoughts have presented themselves to your own notice, and a perception of this order is one of the advantages which belong to the collection of material from personal experience. Whoever has done literary work is likely to have discovered how constantly the literary mind must be on the alert. The daughters of the horse-leech that in the Scriptures are said continually to cry "Give! Give!" are less insatiable than is the greedy pen of the professional writer. Like the grave, it has never enough. He who makes literature a profession must take for his model the barnacle at high tide. As that busy and tireless unpleasantness grasps ceaselessly with finger-like tentacles, so the mind of the writer must be always reaching out,—grasping, grasping, grasping,—until the accumulation of ideas, of facts, of impressions, with the realization that this is literary material, becomes a second nature. Life itself must for the professional writer be so much material. Joy and sorrow, hope, disappointment, whatever he sees and feels, must yield him something which he may set down in words for the instruction or the delight of others. It is not that his feelings are less genuine than those of others; it is not that he writes of his emotions as if they were his own; it is simply that a sort of sub-consciousness takes note always of the world around him and of the world within him no less, seizing all fact and emotion as stuff for the web it weaves.

And here, at the risk of setting down a platitude, it may be well to say that it seems to me of the utmost importance that the professional writer, and especially the young aspirant for literary honors, keep a note-book. It is as foolish to start upon a literary career without the habit of jotting things down as it would be to put to sea without water in the casks. The need is especially great if one is going into any sort of journalistic work, because there is always danger of being called upon to produce "copy" without warning and without material offered either by the editor or by circumstances. There is at such times a great practical value in a well-filled note-book, while the moral support is perhaps of importance even greater. No man who has had literary experience will fail, I believe, to realize the folly of trusting to memory to hold and to bring forward at the right time the thoughts, the reflections, or the facts which come to one unexpectedly. The memory is apt to be a careless servant. It mislays, it injures, it mars the things which are intrusted to it. It is necessary to acquire the habit of setting thoughts down, and of setting them down at once. Do not delude yourself with the notion that you will recall in the morning the clever phrase or acute deduction which your brain evolves after you are tucked safely into bed at night; that you can put upon paper at the end of the journey the incident which struck you in traveling. You may remember to make the record later, but a thought is like a sunset,— the instant it reaches its full glory it begins to fade. What is written while it is fresh has a vitality, a spontaneity which nothing can have that is recalled and set down later. If you are reading and the thought of the author suggests a reflection, throws a sudden illumination upon some spot in your mind hitherto in darkness, do not wait to finish the chapter, but interrupt your reading to write it down. It is a bother. No reader likes to break off to use pencil and note-book,—but the professional writer is forbidden to consider whether he like a thing or not, if it will assist his progress. The first thing in his life is his art,— moral questions aside,—and to this he is to sacrifice everything.

Of the cultivation of the habit of observing, one is almost ashamed to say anything, so often has this been discussed. Every one who discourses upon this subject has spoken of the prime necessity of training the faculties of observation; yet every one who shall discourse hereafter is likely to be called upon to say the same thing. Remember that if you lack material for writing, the fault is entirely your own. The world is around you, infinite and inexhaustible; the question is whether you take what is at hand. Our daily walks and ways afford us all that is needed—except the eye to see and the heart to understand.

Yesterday—which you remember was a sharply cold day—I had occasion to go down town. I noticed at least three things any one of which a clever writer might make the theme of a charming little essay. I saw in the street-car a large, middle-aged man, coarsely dressed, and of rather a forbidding face. He was seated in a corner, and gave an impression of surly ill-nature. A little, thin, weazened lad of not more than six or seven, with pinched features and starved look, poorly clad, and seeming to have been always cold or hungry when he was not both, came in and took the seat next to this man. There was nothing to indicate that the two knew each other, and indeed the boy's air showed plainly enough that they did not; but when the poor forlorn little fellow blew on his small, grimy fists, in vain attempt to warm them, the big, sulky-looking man put out a great hand hardly cleaner, took the boy's blue fingers between his palms, and held them there to warm them. His grim face hardly relaxed, but the kindliness of the act, and the queer mingling of astonishment and pleasure on the child's face, made the incident good to see.

Again, on Washington Street I passed a woman in Quaker garb, who stood looking in at the window of a jeweler. She regarded placidly, yet with an inscrutable look, the gems on velvet cushions within. What she was thinking it would not be easy to say; but what a delightful essay Charles Lamb might have written "On a Quakeress looking in at a Jeweler's Window"!

Half an hour later I passed the silk counter of one of the large dry-goods stores. There a couple of nuns were selecting a sumptuous white brocade, examining it with an air serious and absorbed, and yet subtilely suggestive of feminine delight in the beauty of the stuff. What to them were the pomps and vanities of this world that their taste should be concerned in a purchase so incongruous? Did they buy a new robe wherein the image of some Madonna is to shine forth in splendor at the coming Christmastide, or the garment which some young novice shall wear at her mystic spousals with the church, thenceforth to know no raiment but the strait livery of the sisterhood?

I grant you that one does not chance upon three things so suggestive as these in every trip down town; but there is always something. Learn to see and to hear. Seeing and hearing are more matters of the brain than of eye and ear. Train the mind to observe, and no less train it to phrase; then the whole question of material is settled. Exposition demands, of course, the exercise of reason as well as of observation, but the two are closely bound together; and the mind which is trained to see is as sure to reason about what it sees as the plant which thrusts its rootlets into rich soil is to grow.

XII

Argument

It is one of the most trying conditions of human life that conviction is not proof. It is hard to be brought face to face with the fact that the most ardent belief does not make a thing true. We have most of us known moments when it seemed that there could be no justice in the universe because some hope or some faith which we have cherished with the whole soul was found after all to be but a delusion. Truth in this world must be tried not by desire but by reason; and we can hardly be too careful in studying the processes by which reason attempts its proofs.

Argument has been defined as the endeavor to establish the truth or the falsity of an idea or a proposition. Naturally a written argument is supposed to be addressed to others, but the methods used in constructing it are those which we employ in examining a theory or a proposition in our own minds. It is necessary to study these for the sake of using them in composition; yet it is of no less importance that we apply their principles to our thinking. It may seem to you that I have a tendency to treat English Composition as if it involved the whole duty of man, but it is certainly true that the advantages of familiarity with legal processes may be very great, not only intellectually, but ethically. Since conviction is not proof, either in things emotional or things ethical any more than in things intellectual, it follows that it is essential to be provided with the means of testing the many propositions and ideas which life puts before us. It is not my intention to discuss Argument as a means of spiritual advancement, yet it is not amiss to call attention to its great value, even for one who never intends to write at all.

Looking at Argument simply as a division of composition, we need not have difficulty in perceiving its importance. No intellectual necessity is more common than that of endeavoring to make others think or believe as we think or believe. The effort to establish truth by argument is one which from the dawn of civilization has occupied the best powers of mankind. Openly, in avowed reasoning, or covertly, in cunningly disguised forms, those who write are constantly arguing for one theory or another, for some idea, for some conviction. The writer who is trained to the craft of logic has the same advantage in discussion with one who has not that a trained boxer has in an encounter with a green hand.

It must be evident to any one that Argument is closely allied to Exposition. Much discussion may be resolved into a dispute over definitions, and when thinkers disagree it is more often about terms than about principles. It has happened before now that men have gone to the stake upon a question whether a thing in regard to which everybody was in substantial accord should be called by one name or by another; and it is evident that Exposition may sometimes be more effectively convincing than formal Argument, since if a truth is clearly set forth it is likely to carry conviction with it.

Macaulay's "Machiavelli," which we have examined, goes very near the line of Argument, since, as has been said, it is essentially an endeavor to prove that the vices of the Italians of the fifteenth century were national rather than personal and individual. Indeed, in perhaps the majority of expositions of any complexity there is likely to be an underlying basis of argument. It is difficult to suppose a logical sequence of facts or ideas which does not involve argumentative reasoning, at least tacitly. Here, as everywhere in composition, one form passes into another, and no arbitrary line of division can be drawn. Exposition and Argument are constantly united; and moreover it is true that the latter is constantly given the guise of the former, so that at first glance a chain of logical reasoning is easily mistaken for a simple statement of facts. To quote once more from the "Machiavelli:"—

When war becomes the trade of a separate class, the least dangerous course left to a government is to form a standing army. It is scarcely possible that men can pass their lives in the service of one state without feeling some interest in its greatness. Its victories are their victories. Its defeats are their defeats. The contract loses something of its mercantile character. The services of the soldier are considered as the effects of patriotic zeal, his pay as the tribute of national gratitude. To betray the power which employs him, to be even remiss in its service, are in his eyes the most atrocious and degrading of crimes.

This is a complete argument, easily reducible to logical terms. It opens with the proposition that if war becomes a trade the nation should enlist and control the army; and the remainder of the paragraph is taken up with the proof of this statement. It is not all expressed; but it may be said to consist of three propositions supported as follows:—

First: Men who make war a trade are likely to betray a country.

Men likely to betray are a danger.

Hence, men who make war a trade are a danger.

Second:Men in standing army become identified with the country.

Men identified with the country less likely to betray.

Hence, men in standing army less likely to betray.

Third: Whatever most decreases chance of betrayal is best.

To form standing army most decreases the chance of betrayal.

Hence, to form standing army is best, or least dangerous.

This illustrates how intricately interwoven is Argument with other forms of composition, and how easily one may overlook the fact that he is reading or writing it.

Formally speaking, the difference between Exposition and Argument is the difference between peace and war. One is a hidden and the other an avowed struggle. In Exposition the writer declares; in Argument he defends. In the former there is no necessary endeavor to convince.

The writer concerns himself with setting forth facts, views, or theories; he nominally deals with statement pure and simple. In the latter he attempts to enforce assent to his proposition; to convince is his declared and primary object. Exposition is the teacher; Argument, the soldier.

The danger of Argument is that of all contest. To make an effort to effect a given thing, to endeavor to enforce a view, is of course to expose one's self to the chance of arousing opposition. It is to invite attack, and to run the risk of defeat. For this reason it is necessary to use not a little shrewdness in deciding whether it is best to put what one has to say into the form of declared argument. Often it is wiser to endeavor to produce an exposition so clear that it shall carry with it the conclusion which the writer desires to establish. It is at least safe to assert that in writings meant to convince, the more fully the appearance of not arguing can be maintained the more satisfactory will be the effect. The reader will certainly go as far as he can be made to suppose himself and not the author to be drawing conclusions. Most editorial argumentative writing, and especially that which deals with political questions, is almost of necessity disguised in a semblance as close to Exposition as possible. Where passion is aroused, prejudices excited, and the mind of the reader armed against attempts to convince, whatever is done must be done in a way calculated to soothe rather than to excite.

When Argument avowed and formal is attempted, no pains should be spared to make it irresistible. Reasoning which does not succeed is the strongest presumption against the proposition it seeks to defend. Indeed, logic which fails seems almost to establish the truth of the opposite proposition. "He that taketh the sword shall fall by the sword," and he who advances an argument must either prevail by it or fall altogether. The proposition which before it is argued is viewed at worst with indifference is discredited and disbelieved when once an attempt to establish its credibility has been made and has failed.

The strength of an argument lies in that quality which is called logical accuracy. To cover the whole subject of reasoning minutely it would be necessary to go over the entire field of formal logic; but here we must content ourselves with considering points which are essential and which pretty fairly cover the needs of argumentative composition in a literary sense.

Before beginning a chain of reasoning it is wise to fix what is named the burden of proof. In other words it is well to decide how much one is called upon to prove. It is important to know whether the presumption lies for or against the proposition at issue, to be clear what may be assumed. In many cases this has no especial practical bearing, but it is well to be sure where one stands. It is always easier to defend than to attack, and in so far as a writer can put from him the burden of proof, in so far he has rendered his task lighter. The received theory and the existing state of things have in their favor a presumption which may be advanced by him who argues in their favor and which must always be done away with by him who reasons against them. The writer who attacks civilization, for instance, who decries the existing religion or the value of literature, has upon him the burden of proof; while he who defends them has the advantage of an affirmative assumption. The former is called upon to produce arguments to prove his claim; the latter need do no more than to refute the reasoning of his opponent. On the one hand it is a question of attack; while on the other it is a matter of defense.

The first thing in establishing a line of argument is to define clearly the proposition to be proved. Nothing further can be done until the writer has made the question at issue clear beyond all possibility of mistake. It is necessary to force one's own mind to an understanding so sharp and exact that confusion is impossible. The most common failing of mankind is mental ambiguity; and nothing is more frequent than for writers to be entirely mistaken in what they suppose themselves to mean. The whole so-called Socratic method of reasoning—the most teasingly irritating form of logic ever devised; the Spanish-fly form of conviction—consists chiefly in badgering an opponent into a realization of the fact that he does not know what he is talking about; that he is entirely wrong in his notion of his own meaning. The philosopher who in these less patient days should devote himself to questioning so vexing as that with which Socrates is said to have roasted opponents in his time would run imminent risk of a broken head; but the class of illogical arguers against whom he contended is with us to this day.

Once the proposition is clear in the mind, it is necessary to find means to convey it to the understanding of others; to convey it, be it remembered, so that it shall arrive with meaning and sharpness of outline unimpaired. It is the old question of Clearness. An idea which leaves one mind with all the beauty and symmetry of a snow-crystal often gets to another mind as a mere formless drop of snow-water. To the end that the proposition come to the reader with the identity and form uninjured, it is often needful to declare at the outset the sense in which are used the words, terms, and phrases which follow. The only sure way of dealing with a doubtful case is to say plainly: "When such a word is introduced, it means exactly this." In close writing such defining is almost always essential to the success of the work. You may remember, as an illustration, how Ruskin defines his terms at the beginning of "Modern Painters." In this way only is it possible to avoid the pitfalls which the varied meanings of the language spread for the foot of the unwary. Some of the many possible errors are dangerous, some easily detected. No one, for instance, need be fooled by a fallacy like the following:—

An artist is an interpreter of the beautiful.

Mr. Rothschild's *chef* is an artist.

Hence, Mr. Rothschild's *chef* is an interpreter of the beautiful.

There may be those whose respect for gastronomy is so high that they would not shrink from this conclusion, but taking the argument as it stands, it is evident that the word "artist" is used in a double sense. In the first assertion it signifies one who labors in what we call the fine arts; one gifted with that incommunicable power of which we spoke at the beginning of these talks. In the second assertion, the word "artist" signifies one clever and skillful in the practice of his profession.

To take a more serious illustration, the much mooted question whether Walt Whitman is or is not a poet can be argued only after an agreement upon the sense in which "poet" is to be understood. If "poet" means one who writes verse in metrical forms, the proposition cannot be even discussed, because the fact that Whitman did not write formal metrical verse is admitted by everybody. If, on the other hand, the term "poet" be extended to include writers of imaginative and dithyrambic prose, a discussion becomes almost inevitable. Most of the magazine essays which nominally deal with the question stated are really occupied chiefly with the inquiry, "What sense shall we give to the term 'poet'?"

It is true that the ordinary reader will often fail to make a distinction of this sort. If he be told that the point at issue is Whitman's poetic standing, he will generally accept the statement, however widely the discussion may depart from the proposition. It might seem to follow that it is of little consequence whether a writer is logical or not; but it is always to be remembered that the fact that a reader does not know by what means he is impressed does not necessarily weaken the impression. Indeed, it is probably true that those who are least aware of the processes of literature are often those most vividly affected by them. The writer who has command of literary forms, who understands clearly what he desires to do and how it is best done, will reach and control the mind of the reader, and need not be disturbed by the fact that the latter does not in the least appreciate the art which has seized and which holds him.

It is of the highest importance to keep in mind when defining propositions or terms that the basis of all discussion must be mutually accepted by writer and reader. Until a starting-point where these two are in accord is found, it is manifestly idle to attempt to draw inferences. The writer who argues with the view of convincing the general public is forced to take as premises truth universally allowed, and facts generally known or which can be supported by easily convincing evidence. He is at the outset met with the difficulty that words are seldom free from ambiguity, and that fact and fiction are as inextricably intertangled as are the rootlets of two trees growing side by side. The nicest judgment must be used in determining how far any statement is admittedly true; not, be it noted, how far it *is* true, but how far common consent admits its verity. The premise of any argument addressed to the general reader can go no farther than general conviction goes. Even here a writer is often hampered by the fact that the sense of ambiguity is apt to cling to any question concerning which there has been dispute. This is especially true of subjects about which there has been extensive controversy. It is admitted by everybody, for instance, that there are things in Scripture which are not to be accepted with absolute literalness; yet to assume this in argument is almost inevitably to arouse suspicion if not opposition. No matter how carefully the writer endeavors to keep within bounds of common belief, the uncertainty and the doubt which belong to the proposition in its extreme are apt to interfere with its being given even the weight which it may deserve when carefully guarded.

The best guides here are two: that homely, domestic angel of the mind which we call common sense, and the sincere desire to arrive at and to establish the truth, as distinguished from eagerness to win in argument. If a writer can divest himself of a wish to prevail even if wrongfully, he has increased tenfold his chance of winning rightly. If he can bring his mind to the attitude of simple, unsophisticated truth-seeking, without affectation and without vanity, he is in the best possible condition for arguing successfully. Enthusiasm tells in this as in any other form of composition; but Argument is primarily an appeal to the intellect, and since the reason of the reader is aroused to meet the logic advanced, the writer has need of all his coolness and self-control in devising and arranging his arguments.

The choice of the line of proof which is to be employed is one of the most delicate matters connected with this form of composition. If one undertakes to convince, it is evident that no means which may secure conviction should be slighted; and it is of importance to select the train of reasoning along which the mind of the reader will move with the least opposition. Here advice cannot avail much. The student must depend upon care, good judgment, and practice, with the study and analysis of the masterpieces of reasoning. The choice of methods in arguing is the selection of the order of battle; on it depends much of the success alike of attack and of defense.

The sense of the proposition, the meaning of the terms, and the line of argument having been determined, they must be held to firmly to the end. No defect in disputation is more common than that of shifting ground. Sometimes, especially in debate, this is deliberate. A clever dialectician, one who is able deftly to twist words to varied uses and to turn phrases about, has little difficulty, if he finds himself cornered, in altering his position completely. He easily confuses the terms so that the point at issue is changed. He raises a cloud of phrases under cover of which his attack is shifted to another quarter, as a line of battle is sometimes altered behind a cloud of smoke. This is less often possible in written conflict than in oral, yet there it may sometimes be done. It is at best, however, merely a temporization. What is set down in "the cold permanence of print" may be examined until its inaccuracies are brought to light. The swiftness of speech and the glamour of personal persuasiveness will cover fallacies which could avail nothing if put upon paper. Any change of position, moreover, is a confession of weakness; and once it is observed, the effect of the entire chain of reasoning is weakened, if not destroyed altogether.

A change of base in argument is the result of deliberate intention less often than of mental confusion. Few of us realize how seldom we think clearly; how much more rarely we think clearly and consecutively; and how most rare it is that we think clearly, consecutively, and logically. Much training is required to bring the mind to the power of holding fast to a single issue in discussion, of persisting in a single line of proof, of resisting all temptations to turn to side issues.

Nor is this solely from a lack of intellectual power; it is in part due to an instinctive desire to escape unwelcome results. One of the surest indications of a firm and well-disciplined mind is that it does not shrink from its own conclusions. The natural, human tendency is to escape from a distasteful result of investigation or reasoning by assuming that the process must be wrong because the decision arrived at is unpleasant. Yet to dislike a proposition is not to disprove it. To protest against the fact established by sound logic no more destroys it than the wail of a child brings down from heaven the round yellow moon for which he cries. All intellectual growth and all character stand upon the willingness of the mind to accept and to act upon the conclusions at which it arrives by the exercise of its best reasoning powers. It is much to be able to think; it is more to dare to think; but it is most of all to be able to accept without shrinking or evasion the results of thought, whether one's own or others'.

XIII

Argumentative Form

It is proper and perhaps even important that the student shall learn the distinction which is made by logicians between reasoning which is inductive and that which is deductive. As a matter of practical work in the writing of arguments, the distinction is of less importance than might seem from the formality with which these terms are treated; but as Induction and Deduction are words which the true logician cannot mention without at least a seeming impulse to cross himself, it is well to know what the difference is.

Induction, then, is reasoning from the particular to the general; the establishment of an hypothesis by showing that the facts agree with it. It is preëminently the scientific method. By observing natural phenomena, the scientist conceives what the law which governs them must be. This idea of the general principle is then the hypothesis which he attempts to prove; and his method is to examine the facts under all conditions possible, establishing his proposition by showing that the facts are in accord with it.

Deduction is the converse of this, and consists in drawing out particular truths from general ones. A universal proposition may be regarded as a bundle in which are bound together many individual ones. It is the work of deduction to take these out,—to separate any one of them from the rest. The general truth, "All metals are elements," includes in it the especial truths, "Iron is an element," "Gold is an element," and so on for each metal which could be named. Deduction is the process of separating one of these from the whole. Speaking broadly, scientific reasoning is more likely to be inductive, while other reasoning is more likely to be deductive.

As a matter of practical composition, Argument is the statement of a proposition, and the arrangement of the proofs which the writer believes will establish its truth. The essential matter is to begin with some truth or fact generally acknowledged, and to lead the mind of the reader on by deductions which cannot be disputed, until the proposition to be proved is reached as an unassailable conclusion.

This process may be very simple, or extremely complex; the steps may be slight, or they may be, like the platforms of the pyramids, barely scalable. In discussing methods, it is necessary to use some technical expressions which it is well to define:—

A Term is a word or combination of words used to name some thing or idea in reasoning.

A Proposition is a statement of the relation between two terms.

If we say, "The man is a patriot," we have a sentence in which is a statement of the relation between the thing "man" and the thing "patriot." This is therefore a proposition. Here the terms are "man" and "patriot," because these are the names of the things of which we speak in reasoning.

We might now make another proposition, this time general, and say, "A patriot is a valuable citizen." Here the terms are "patriot" and "valuable citizen," and the proposition asserts a relation between them.

If these two propositions are examined, they are found to have in common the term "patriot," and it is seen to be possible to draw from them another proposition. If the man of whom mention is made is a patriot, and a patriot is a valuable citizen, it is evident enough that the man must be a valuable citizen. It is merely an application of the principle that things which are equal to the same thing are equal to each other. And this brings us to a third definition:—

A Syllogism is a group of three propositions, of which, if the first two are true, the third must follow as a deduction from them.

A complete syllogism has just been given: The man is a patriot; a patriot is a valuable citizen; hence the man is a valuable citizen.

It is possible to draw a third proposition only from two that have one term in common. It follows that there are three terms in a syllogism,—the first and second propositions having one term alike, and each having a particular term which reappears in the third proposition. This third proposition is that which the endeavor is made to prove. To establish a proposition by syllogism, then, it is necessary to find two others which contain each one of its terms, and which have a term in common. It is necessary to add that not from every pair of propositions which contain a common term is it possible to draw a third, and thus to form a syllogism. If we say, "A rose is a flower," "A lily is a flower," we have two propositions which have a common term, yet we cannot go on to make the third proposition, "Hence a rose is a lily." The term which is common to both propositions must in one of them be spoken of as a whole, or in a general way. Logicians say that it must be "distributed;" in other words, one assertion must cover the term in its entire extent. In the first syllogism which we examined, the common—it is usually called the "middle"—term is in the second proposition spoken of in a general way. "A patriot is a valuable citizen" is an assertion of all patriots. In the false syllogism, "A rose is a flower; a lily is a flower," there is nothing said of all flowers, and yet "flower" is the middle term. The rose is one flower, the lily is one flower, but until there is something said of all flowers it is not possible to draw out a new conclusion,—to form a syllogism.

He who wishes to exercise his wits with pretty mental gymnastics may learn from books on logic that there are a great many varieties of syllogisms. There are twenty-four valid ones, and a crowd of poor relatives, which exist under the discrediting title, "imperfect syllogisms," and which, paradoxically, are of no use until they have been "reduced." When it is added that each has a fine Latin name, the reader may appreciate that he is here being spared a good deal.

Although it is not possible to take space for a very intricate example of the skeleton of an argument, it is hardly fair to give nothing more complex than a simple syllogism; and the following may assist the formation of a more clear conception of the form in which reasoning should be put. Suppose the proposition which is to be proved to be, "The Norsemen discovered America before Columbus."

Taking a few of the more obvious arguments which might be advanced in support of this proposition, and arranging them so as to begin with the more generally allowed and easily proved, we have:

1. The frequent appearance in European literature before Columbus of allusions to a land across the sea.

2. The story in the Icelandic Sagas.

3. Norse remains in America.

These proofs will be sufficient for purposes of illustration. Let us examine them in detail a little. Under each of these proofs—which it is convenient to call subordinate propositions—lies a syllogism, whether it is fully stated or not. The writer must be entirely clear in his own mind what this is, whether it seem to him well to state it explicitly or not. Here the syllogism of the first subordinate proposition, briefly stated, is:—

Allusions to a land over sea prove knowledge of such a land.

In pre-Columbian literature are allusions to land over sea.

Hence there must have been knowledge of such a land.

This brings us face to face with the necessity of supporting premises with facts. To support the first sub-proposition there must be citations from pre-Columbian literature. This is a mere matter of research. One reason for putting this especial proof first is that in supporting it it is possible to begin with facts which cannot be questioned. It is true that the very next step will bring us upon doubtful territory, but we start from firm ground. The moment that the passages are quoted, the possibility occurs to the mind that they may be taken to refer to lands then known, or as the expression of mythical fancies. These objections must be met. An argument can no more pass an unanswered objection than a locomotive can cross a bridge from which a span is missing. Reasons must here be given for connecting with the New World the passages cited. It will be no less important to show the reasons for supposing that the information which the ancient writers possessed of the New World came from the Norsemen. The rest may all be allowed, and yet be held to have no bearing on the thing to be proved, so that this link in the chain must be made strong and evident.

This last point illustrates the sort of questions which are likely to arise in regard to arrangement. Is it well to introduce here the proofs that this knowledge of another continent came from the Norse, or would it be better to wait until the Icelandic Sagas have been spoken of? In the latter case, the parts of the argument may be more closely bound together, and it gives an air of fairness to the whole when the writer is willing to go back a good way in his argument to take up possible objections and answer them. Against this is to be balanced the possibility that the reader may be put into a suspicious state of mind by finding that a doubtful point is passed over, and so be less easily convinced than he otherwise might be. The writer of an argument must consider these things, and upon the good judgment with which he settles such questions much of his success depends.

In this first sub-proposition there is no need of stating formally the syllogism involved, since, if the first or major premise is successfully defended, the rest follows obviously. As a matter of practical arrangement, then, the sub-proposition and its defense might stand in this order:—

1.   The discovery of America by the Norsemen is proved by the allusions in pre-Columbian literature to a land over sea.

    a. Citation of passages.

    b. Proofs that these do not refer to the Eastern Hemisphere.

    c. Proofs that they are not mythical allusions.

    d. Proofs that they do refer to America.

    e. Proofs that the knowledge shown came from Norsemen.

When these points are established, the first sub-proposition, with its underlying syllogism, may be looked upon as proved, and the next may be taken up. I have not studied the question of the discovery of America by the Norsemen closely enough to know that the line of proof given is the best possible, but it serves well enough to illustrate the general form of the skeleton of an argument. Each of the subordinate propositions must be divided and subdivided if necessary, until the divisions can be handled easily and proved conclusively; and the writer will do well to test the strength of his argument by making a complete chain of the syllogisms involved, seeing which rests upon another, so that the arrangement may be conformed to principles of natural sequence.

One important matter in reasoning is never to claim too much. Care must be taken not to put upon a proof a greater strain than it will bear. It is also an obvious rule that it is wise to insist upon no more than is absolutely needed to establish the proposition in hand. Sometimes it is wise to indicate that more might be proved, but in general the assent of the reader is to be treated as a bank account to be drawn upon as far as it is necessary, but in no case beyond the actual need of the occasion. It is well never to waste strength in proving more than is essential, and always to avoid a side issue as one shuns a road leading to sure destruction. Often it is a wise device in argumentation to establish a point and leave the reader to perceive its import. Here as everywhere a thing which the reader is led to do for himself is a hundred fold more effective than anything which can be done or said for him. The phrase, "Is it not possible that these facts prove this?" has won more converts than the boldest assertion: "These proofs make it impossible to doubt." Man that is born of woman is born to obstinacy as the sparks fly upward, and if he be assured that he cannot or shall not doubt, he is apt to begin to doubt from simple contrariety. Yet it will not do to run any risk of leaving the reader in doubt as to what has been established by the arguments given. It is often necessary to insist that a proposition is proved. A victory is hardly recognized as a victory until the trumpets are blown, and an argument is scarcely concluded without some sort of a declaration of success.

Where the line is to be drawn between the extreme of leaving to the reader the perception of what is proved and that of insisting that a demonstration has been made must depend upon the audience addressed. The writer of an argument has especial need to be sure to whom he speaks. He must consider the knowledge of his audience, their views, and especially their prejudices. It is in relation to the last that there comes into play what it has been the fashion to call Persuasion. Although Argument is an appeal to the intellect, there are few chains of reasoning which fail to appeal also to the emotions. It is hardly possible to conceive of a discussion which will not to a greater or less degree touch the passions of those addressed. Much is effected by keeping in mind the natural prejudices of the reader, and so framing arguments that they shall appeal directly to the emotions by the personal or selfish nature of their deductions. An illustration is to be found in political harangues, which, while nominally devoted to proving the wisdom or advisability of some party measure, are really only clever attempts to convince that the measure is for the personal advantage of voters. This is, of course, the abuse of this form of argument. The legitimate use of this appeal to the passions is in the putting of reasoning sound and wholesome in itself into a form which shall captivate the hearer or reader. It is the lavishing upon the composition of all the graces of manner, of style, of ornament, which the writer can compass, to the end that the reader shall be attracted and inclined to accept the conclusions set down. Stevenson speaks of a somewhat different matter in words which are strictly applicable here:—

> Whatever be the obscurities, whatever the intricacies of the argument, the neatness of the fabric must not suffer, or the artist has been proved unequal to his design. And, on the other hand, no form of words must be selected, no knot must be tied among the phrases, unless knot and word be precisely what is wanted to forward and illuminate the argument; for to fail in this is to swindle in the game.—*Cont. Rev.*, vol. xlvii. (1885), p. 551.

Almost as often as with the establishment of our own reasoning, are we concerned in argument with endeavors to overthrow the logic of an opponent. Frequently it is necessary to refute views opposed to that which is being put forward. It is in general wise not to bring this in too soon. It is well to predispose the reader in favor of the conclusion to be defended, and then to take up contrary opinions. Sometimes a broad statement at the beginning to the effect that objections exist is politic; and in any case it is important that there be no slightest appearance of shirking or evading the issue. When the writer is conscious that the weight of popular sentiment or general opinion is against him, he may sometimes command attention and provoke interest by boldly plunging at once into an attack upon commonly received theories. Audacity always commands attention, and if it be reinforced by ability it is no less sure of admiration. A striking example of this method is to be found in Colonel Ingersoll's attacks upon the Bible and religion. However one may be shocked by his violations of good taste, and whether one does or does not agree with his methods or his conclusions, it is impossible to deny his success as a speaker. The very boldness with which he has attacked has insured a hearing. This form of discussion calls for dash, courage, and confidence,—and it is sometimes the result of sheer impudence. Only he who has great powers and perfect command of them can reasonably hope to succeed here.

For answering the arguments of others, and indeed for the proper examination of one's own, it is necessary to give attention to the numerous fallacies which may creep into reasoning, by design or by accident. These are to be completely mastered only by the minute study of logic; but some are so common that they should be considered here.

The first fallacy is that of the confusion of terms, such as that found in the attempt to prove the *chef* to be an interpreter of the beautiful, or in the question whether Whitman was a poet.

The second fallacy which in practical writing it is well to be on guard against is the *non sequitur*. There is much advanced as argument—as for instance in political editorials—where consecutiveness is confounded with causality. *Post hoc ergo propter hoc* is the phrase which sums this up: After this, therefore because of this. "We shall die after eating this meal, therefore this meal is the cause of our death," is an example of this fallacy. Put in this way the absurdity is evident; but a genuine fallacy, lurking under words as the conventional serpent of school-girl compositions and of temperance orators lurks beneath flowers, is a different thing. Here is part of an editorial from one of the leading New York daily journals:

> The vote of Senator X. is a striking illustration of the power of money among the law-makers of this great nation. The vigorous and unscrupulous support which has been given to this bill by Mr. A., the western billionaire, is known to everybody; and equally well known is the fact that hitherto Senator X. has been counted among the stanch opposers of the iniquitous measure. Senator X. is known to have had a private interview with Mr. A. on the evening before the vote was taken, and the result was evident when next morning the Senator gave his support to the bill which he had before steadily opposed.

In the especial case to which this refers there may or there may not have been bribery; but it is well to bear in mind that this editorial proves nothing. It amounts merely to saying that the vote happened after the interview and was therefore the result of it; so that it is in reality one of those fallacies which in a simpler form appear so absurd. Yet readers in abundance accept this sort of thing as proof, especially when political prejudice inclines them to believe it. It would seem that a little common sense and a little care in examination were all that could be needed to dispose of specious errors of this class, yet they every day prevail.

The third fallacy is that of analogy. Analogy proves a probability, but it cannot establish a certainty. If a young woman has refused a dozen suitors, it is manifestly absurd to say that this proves that she will be equally unkind to the thirteenth. Politicians reason by analogy that a State which hitherto has gone Republican or Democratic may be counted upon to give a majority for its old party; when, lo, a change comes suddenly, and the conclusion is found to be false. That we have always liked the novels of a certain author does not insure that we shall be pleased with his next; that the sun has always risen does not prove that it will rise to-morrow morning; that men have from time immemorial been born with one head does not prove that a child may not be born with two,—as testify the freaks of dime museums. It is true that analogy often establishes a probability so strong that it amounts to a moral certainty. We are justified in acting upon the assumption that the sun will rise to-morrow, and in assuming that any given child of whose birth we hear has but one head. It is important in arguing, however, to bear in mind the difference, whether in one's own reasoning or in that of an opponent, between analogy and absolute proof. Things which are like the same thing are like each other; but things that are like the same thing are not necessarily equal to each other.

The practical rules which may be given for the writing of Argument are chiefly recapitulations of what has been said.

a.   Begin with clear understanding and clear statement of proposition and of terms.

b.   Plan argument with reference to the especial point to be established and to the audience to be addressed.

c.   Proceed generally from the more obvious to the less clear, and from the weaker to the stronger proof.

d.   Be acutely alive to fallacies in any reasoning which is to be refuted, but to fallacies in your own work no less.

e.   Never force a proposition or a proof beyond its value.

f.   Concede all side issues and irrelevant matters if by so doing you do not lessen the chain of reasoning in points really important, and especially if in so doing you can foster a disposition favorable to your position.

g.   Always remember that assertion is not argument.

To these rules might not inappropriately be added the saying of Sophocles: "Truth is always the strongest argument."

The practical application of Argument to literary work is not difficult to discover. The most obvious use of this sort of composition is in the plea of the lawyer, the editorials of the newspaper, the essay establishing scientific theories, literary opinions, or the like. Whoever writes at all, however, even if it be but in simple private correspondence, is sure to employ Argument sooner or later, and to a greater or less degree. It may be in defense of a friend, the justification of one's own acts, in proving the value of a new invention, supporting political or scientific views, in urging a particular line of investment,— in short, in any one of a thousand different ways. In one shape or another, reasoning comes constantly into play. He is merely a "mush of concession" who never attempts to bring another to his way of thinking. Indeed, he who does not endeavor to make others think as he thinks may be suspected of never thinking at all. Life is a continuous conflict, the strife for the survival of the fittest. The instinct to make our opinions prevail is in the blood of the meekest. Civilization differs from barbarism chiefly in that the strife has become intellectual instead of physical; and intellectual conflict is but another name for Argument. Since our lot is cast in a civilized state of society, to neglect this form of composition is to neglect the manual of arms of the battalion in which Fate has enrolled us!

XIV

Description

Description is at once the most common and the most difficult of the varieties of composition. It is apparently a thing which nobody fears to undertake, while it is certainly one which only a master is able to do really well. Everybody attempts it, yet there are probably in literature fewer fully successful descriptions than there are examples of any other sort of writing whatever.

A description is an endeavor to call up before the mind of the reader a picture of the thing described. Nothing is easier than to make a catalogue of things which one has seen; to schedule the details of a landscape, the particulars of a building, a room or a person. To convey a clear and accurate idea of the whole is most difficult. The untrained writer is apt to make of his attempts at description a mere running memorandum of points which he remembers in a scene. He sets down a list of matters more or less important, not because he can thus make the whole vivid and real to the reader, but because they are true. The result is that he has forced the truth to convey a falsehood—if indeed it be made to convey anything intelligible.

No student can go far in the examination of any of the arts without discovering that the object of expression is not so much to tell the truth as to produce an impression of truth. The literal truth may easily give a false impression, and becomes in that case the most vicious of falsehoods of which art is capable, just as the telling of facts with intent to deceive is the most dangerous form of lying. The thing to be sought is not accuracy of statement, but accuracy of perception, and the means must be subordinated to the effect.

It follows that even more vitally important than that all details be true, is that they be significant; that they not only appeal to the memory or the reason of the writer, but that they have a creative effect upon the mind of the reader. The author may remember that all the things which he sets down are true, yet it may be that all which he writes is false in its result. In morals it is fitting that we give credit for good intentions, no matter what the result of them may be; in authorship the intention is of no consequence whatever. The result is the only thing to be taken into account. Here to fail is to fail, whether one meant well or ill; and from this there is no escape.

I am of course keeping strictly to the definition of Description which has been given. In that form of Exposition which is frequently called Description, the giving a scientific or practical account of a thing, accuracy of detail is of the first importance. If one is called upon to "describe" a machine, it is not usually meant that he shall try to present to the mind a picture of it, but that he shall expound it. This is not Description in a literary sense, and with this we have nothing now to do. In the sense in which the term is used as naming a department of composition, Description is not scientific, but emotional; not categorical, but literary; not intellectual, so much as visual. The description of a landscape falls short of its intent just so far as it fails to call up before the inner eye the image which was before the mind of the writer,—save in so far as from the nature of language any word-picture must fall short. If a passage designed to paint a scene does not make the reader seem actually to see that scene it cannot be held that the author has fulfilled his intention.

It must be recognized once and for all that words cannot really paint. No artificer can labor intelligently until he has learned not only the possibilities but also the limitations of the means at his disposal. In writing it is important to remember what words cannot do as well as what they can effect. The most that the writer can hope to do is to revive in the mind of the reader images which the latter has seen. In speaking of the limitations of language in the first of these talks, I reminded you that when we read the description of a landscape we construct an image out of material already in the mind. Words cannot paint; that is the province of another art. The painter is able to present fresh forms, colors, combinations, new landscapes, strange and unknown figures, and all varieties of visual novelty. The writer must content himself with a reawakening and a rearrangement of forms, figures, colors, images, already in the reader's mind. His effect of novelty must come from fresh and untried combinations; from the vividness with which he is able to arouse these remembered images until they appear so real as to seem new.

It easily follows that the writer who understands his art will cunningly avail himself of images which are likely to be stored in the minds of his readers. It is the same principle which directs us to appeal to common emotions, to the general experiences of mankind.[5] Let us examine a little this extract from an account of a walk in the woods in England:—

> "Looking between the trees, I saw a little circular glade, two or three score feet across. It was covered with soft, thin grass, speckled with palely blue scabiosas, and set round with tall, slender trees. On one side was a strange imitation of the great trilith at Stonehenge, formed by two tall boulders across which had fallen the trunk of a large beech tree."

In America the reader might not know what scabiosas are, but as this was written in England, where, in some parts at least, the pale

---

5   A pleasant if a little exaggerated illustration of the way in which pictures are made up from materials in the mind is afforded by this account of the vision of Rome which a boy conjured up in his mind: "Rome! ... I tried to imagine what it would be like when I got there. The Coliseum I knew, of course, from a woodcut in the history-book; so to begin with I plumped that down in the middle. The rest had to be patched up from the little gray market-town where twice a year we went to have our hair cut; hence, in the result, Vespasian's amphitheatre was approached by muddy little streets, wherein the Red Lion and the Blue Boar, with Somebody's Entire along their front, and "Commercial Room" on their windows; the doctor's house, of substantial red brick; and the façade of the New Wesleyan Chapel, which we thought very fine, were the chief architectural ornaments; while the Roman populace pottered about in smocks and corduroys, twisting the tails of the Roman calves and inviting each other to beer in musical Wessex."— KENNETH GRAHAM: *The Golden Age.*

blue blossoms of the flower are common in every field, the audience addressed would probably not be puzzled by this word. It is to be supposed that even there, however, there would be many who would fail to feel any force in the phrase "the great trilith at Stonehenge." A few might have seen it, and others might be familiar with pictures representing it; but the chance of finding this image in the mind of the reader was so small as to render its use at least ill-advised; and especially so as the comparison is that of a trifling thing to a great one. The reader who recalled Stonehenge would be likely to feel that there was small excuse for likening a tree trunk tumbled across a couple of boulders to the magnificent and mysterious monuments of Salisbury Plain.

An example of the fact that even in dealing with the supernatural a writer has no resource save images already known may be found in any story dealing with the weird. Take this from Rudyard Kipling's tale, "The Return of Imray," where the spirit of a murdered man is haunting the house:—

> We were alone in the house, but none the less it was too fully occupied by a tenant with whom I did not wish to interfere. I never saw him, but I could see the curtain between the rooms quivering where he had just passed through; I could hear the chairs creaking as the bamboos sprung under a weight that had just quitted them; and I could feel when I went to get a book from the dining-room that somebody was waiting in the shadows of the front veranda till I should have gone away.

This is perhaps not one of Mr. Kipling's happiest passages, since it insists somewhat too strongly upon the corporeal bulk of the phantom, but it illustrates the point which we are considering.

Of the greatest importance in Description is the point of view. First there is the question of the physical point of view. The writer must know certainly and clearly at what point he has placed the reader to look at the landscape, the person, or the scene which is described. In the first lecture I quoted the description which opens Kingsley's "Westward Ho!" There the point of view is that of one approaching the "little white town of Bideford," but there is at the very outset a violation of propriety which injures the force of the whole. "The little white town of Bideford," the author says, "which slopes upward from its broad tide-river paved with yellow sands, and many-arched old bridge where salmon wait for Autumn floods." The "yellow sands" and the salmon are details which are known to one familiar with the town, but they are not apparent to the stranger, they are not evident from the point of view chosen, and their introduction at once confuses the impression.

Goethe, who was keenly alive to all the details of literary workmanship, commented upon a passage in Scott which violates the point of view. In talking with Eckermann he said:—

It is a peculiarity of Walter Scott's that his great talent in representing details often leads him into faults. Thus in "Ivanhoe," there is a scene where they are seated at a table in a castle-hall, at night, and a stranger enters. Now, he is quite right in describing the stranger's appearance and dress, but it is a fault that he goes to the length of describing his feet, shoes, and stockings. When we sit down in the evening and some one comes in, we notice only the upper part of his body. If I describe the feet, daylight enters at once, and the scene loses its nocturnal character.— March 11, 1831.

The point of view may of course be progressive. The reader may be led on through a landscape or through the rooms of a house, for instance. In this it is necessary to keep clearly in mind and to make evident to the reader every alteration in the point of sight. Properly used, this method may be very effective; but the least vagueness inevitably leads to confusion. No description can be successful if there is any uncertainty in regard to the station of observation. The reader must know where he is looking from as well as what he is at. He may not, it is true, realize this, but the writer must realize it for him.

What has been said of the physical point of view may be applied to the emotional. The feeling of the spectator influences the impression made upon him by that at which he looks. Do not forget the mood in which you expect your reader to see the mental picture which you are endeavoring to present. If you introduce into the midst of a highly wrought and exciting tale a description of a scene so closely connected with the narrative that it is important for the reader to see it clearly, you have to consider that if you have the hold you should have upon him he is aroused by the story, and will look with quickened eyes upon the view your words present. You may therefore give him, quickly and sharply, details such as imprint themselves on the brain in moments of excitement. The principle is one so obvious as hardly to need further illustration; but it is not to be looked upon as of small importance because small space is here given to it.

Much modern description may be said to be entirely emotional, in the sense that it aims rather to produce the emotions aroused by a scene than to picture the scene in its physical aspect. A recognition of the difficulty of presenting a visual image has brought this about, just as it has brought about the discarding of the old-time fashion of cataloguing details. The modern heroine, for instance, is seldom described by the best novelists. Two or three characteristic particulars are generally considered sufficient to suggest the whole, or one touch is cunningly added to another in the body of the narrative, so that the image is formed almost imperceptibly.

It is convenient to consider Description as being of two sorts, although no sharp line can be drawn between them. One method may be called Direct Description, and the other Suggestive Description.

The names indicate the distinction,—an attempt to call up a picture by the enumeration directly of the characteristics of an object or a scene, or to suggest it by an imaginative figure. The former is the simpler, the more common, the less subtle. The difference between these sorts of description may perhaps be appreciated by contrasting two passages, the first from Shelley's "Mont Blanc," and the second from Coleridge's "Hymn before Sunrise in the Vale of Chamouni." Shelley, dealing directly with his subject, and enumerating actual features of the scene, writes:—

Thus thou, Ravine of Arve—dark, deep Ravine—

Thou many-colored, many-voicèd vale,

> Over whose pines and crags and caverns sail
>
> Fast cloud-shadows and sunbeams.

Coleridge, on the other hand, suggests a picture rather than gives one directly:—

> Hast thou a charm to stay the morning star
>
> In his steep course? So long he seems to pause
>
> On thy bald, awful head, O sovran Blanc!

In the one case there is a statement of particulars, and from these separate features the reader is expected to build up the scene before his mental vision. In the other there is merely a suggestion of the morning star hovering lingeringly over the snowy, awe-inspiring crest of the mighty mountain. It seems to me that in this especial instance Coleridge, for once at least, has the better of Shelley, and that the implied picture is more vivid and effective than the picture more carefully elaborated.

To take an illustration from prose, let us contrast the description which Dickens gives of Sairey Gamp with that of Mrs. Fezziwig. Of the former he says:—

She was a fat old woman, this Mrs. Gamp, with a husky voice and a moist eye, which she had a remarkable power of turning up and only showing the white of it.[6] Having very little neck, it cost her some trouble to look over herself, if one may say so, at those to whom she talked. She wore a very rusty gown, rather the worse for snuff, and a shawl and bonnet to correspond.... The face of Mrs. Gamp—the nose in particular—was red and swollen; and it was difficult to enjoy her society without becoming conscious of a smell of spirits.

Of the other lady Dickens merely remarks:—

In came Mrs. Fezziwig, one vast substantial smile.

Good as the former of these descriptions is of its kind, it seems to me that if this were all that we were told about these two characters,

6   Sic.

we should have in the mind a more distinct picture of Mrs. Fezziwig than of Mrs. Gamp. One is not obliged to share this opinion, however, to appreciate the difference between the two methods.

In Direct Description, the first thing to be considered, after the point of view is selected, is what is the central idea of the picture which is to be produced. It is apt to be the fact that from a description the reader gets one clear and vivid impression to which all else is subordinate, and beside which all else is comparatively vague. It is therefore often wise to put all the real stress upon the points to be accented, leaving the reader to imagine the rest.

The matter of selecting the central thought is of the more weight, since it is important that this be given clearly to the reader at its first presentation. Whoever has tried to alter a mental image knows how difficult it is to change a picture which is already defined in the imagination. If the mind in constructing a picture has conceived of a mountain as standing on the right, and afterward finds that the author intended it to be on the left, it is on the right that that mountain is likely to remain in the ideal landscape. I have always been a little troubled by the fact that in his description at the commencement of "The Merry Men," Stevenson, careful and exquisite artist though he was, speaks of the "great granite rocks that ... go down together in troops into the sea, like cattle on a summer's day;" and then, a little later, declares that "on calm days you can go wandering between them in a boat for hours, echoes following you about the labyrinth." From the comparison to cattle, I always get the idea of boulders much smaller than the second sentence shows to have been intended. The readjustment is an unpleasant break which jars upon the reality of the whole.

In the first example which I gave you, we are told that the writer saw a glade, covered with soft, thin grass, speckled with flowers. It is added that the glade was set round with trees, and then that on one side were a couple of tall boulders, across which had fallen a large beech tree. This does not seem the natural or the effective order. The eye would first notice that the glade was set about with trees, next that there was the large fallen tree, lying across the boulders, and only after this see that the ground was covered with flower-spotted, thin grass.

Here is another example which illustrates the same error:—

Vervain saw before him a rude mob, armed with all sorts of improvised weapons. They had evidently caught up scythes, bill-hooks, axes, or whatever came first to hand. In the midst of them his eye distinguished Henley and Western, and they were all led by a large, coarse man with a red cap, who seemed to have some authority over them. They were marshaled into a rude order, the lines being wavering and uneven, and all were evidently fiercely excited.

The author speaks first of a "rude mob," a phrase which calls up a formless and confused mass of men. We are next told that in the midst the spectator recognized two acquaintances, then that there was a leader, and after that that the crowd was moving in rude order, with uneven lines. This last statement forces the reader to alter, if he can, his first impression, and instead of imagining a confused crowd, to think of a company irregularly organized. If the writer had really seen in his own mind the thing of which he wrote, he would in the first place have spoken of the mob as a company led by a leader conspicuous in his red cap, and marching in wavering lines. After this he would have been conscious of the rough and improvised weapons, and only after all these things had forced themselves upon his attention would there have been any recognition of individuals.

To select the central idea it is generally safe to consider what one's own first or strongest impression was or would be at sight of the thing pictured. The effective order is usually that which would be the actual experience of the reader if he were standing in the flesh at the point of view indicated by the author. This is the natural method, and while it has its dangers, it is at once practical and logical. In any case, there must be some reason for the order, so that the reader may be led from one point to the next. Consecutiveness is the logic of Description and Narration.

As an example of describing where the details are arranged as they would be likely to catch the attention of the spectator, we may take this picture from that classic of American literature, Sylvester Judd's "Margaret:"—

The pond covered several hundreds of acres, its greatest diameter measuring about a mile and a half; its outline was irregular, here divided by sharp rocks, there retreating into shaded coves; and on its face appeared three or four small islands, bearing trees and low bushes. Its banks, if not really steep, had a bluff and precipitous aspect from the tall forest that girdled it about.—Ch. i.

Or this exquisite bit from Stevenson:—

The river there is dammed back for the service of the flour-mill just below, so that it lies deep and darkling, and the sand slopes into brown obscurity with a glint of gold; and it has but newly been recruited by the borrowings of the snuff-mill just above, and these, tumbling merrily in, shake the pool to its black heart, fill it with drowsy eddies, and set the curded froth of many other mills solemnly steering to and fro upon the surface.—*The Manse.*

Dickens observes this natural order in many of his detailed pictures of persons. The portrait of Mr. Grimwig may serve as an example:—

At this moment there walked into the room, supporting himself by a thick stick, a stout old gentleman, rather lame in one leg, who was dressed in a blue coat, striped waistcoat, nankeen breeches and gaiters, and a broad-brimmed white hat with the sides turned up with green. A very small-plaited shirt-frill stuck out from his waistcoat, and a very long steel watch-chain, with nothing but a key at the end, dangled loosely below it. The ends of his white neckerchief were twisted into a ball about the size of an orange; the variety of shapes into which his countenance was twisted defy description. He had a manner of screwing his head round on one side when he spoke, and looking out of the corners of his eyes at the same time, which irresistibly reminded the beholder of a parrot.—*Oliver Twist.*

This elaboration of particulars is somewhat out of fashion. Particulars are grasped by the eye so quickly that the deliberation of words is apt to destroy proportion, while it is also true that the reader is in danger of forgetting the beginning before he reaches the end.

It is perhaps worth while to give an example of the abuse of this method, since all inexperienced writers have a tendency to mistake a catalogue for a description. It is manifestly idle to pile up particulars, unless they are kept subordinate to some central thought. Here is the description of the heroine of a modern English novel, "A Chelsea Householder:"—

To begin, then, Muriel was tall, with a slight, erect figure, a quick step, and an air of youth and vigor which did the beholder good to look at.[7] Her face was oval, as nearly oval at least as a face can be in which the chin is a good deal more pronounced than is usual in classic beauties. The cheeks were pale, paler than they had any business to be, judging by the rest of the physique, the most noticeable fact in point of coloring being that the eyes, hair, brows, and lashes were all of the same, or pretty nearly the same, color—a deep, dark brown, inclining to chestnut above the temples, from which the hair was brushed courageously back, so as to form a small knot at the back of the head. Her eyes—not, perhaps, by the way, a strikingly original trait in a heroine—were large and bright; indeed, brighter or pleasanter eyes have seldom looked out of a woman's face, their beauty consisting less in their size and color than in this very vividness and brightness, which seemed to shine out of the irises themselves. For all that, the face in repose was not exactly a bright one, or rather the brightness came to it only by fits and starts, its prevailing expression being a somewhat sober one, a sobriety giving way, however, at a touch, and being replaced by a peculiarly sunshiny smile and glance.

This is not the whole of the paragraph, but it is enough for our purpose. There need not be a better example of how not to do it, or of how much may be said about a thing without conveying any definite idea of it. For my own part, I have no idea whatever how Muriel looked, and long before I got half through her verbal portrait I had

---

7   *Sic*

ceased to care. Few faults are more common than this furnishing a list of particulars in the expectation that the reader will construct therefrom the picture which the author has not been clever enough to make clear—a method, it might be added, not unlike the system of punctuation adopted by the late so-called Lord Timothy Dexter, who put all the points together at the end of his book, and directed his readers to distribute them at their own pleasure.

It is hardly needful to remark upon the prime necessity of clearness in description, but it is perhaps not amiss to remind beginners that it is not possible to picture a thing which the writer does not himself see. If he is writing of an imaginary landscape and speak of a tree, he should be able if he choose to count the branches of that tree as clearly as if it in reality stood before him. Unless he know whether the heads of the flowers tip to the right or to the left, whether the sheep on the hillside of which he writes are nearer the fence on the one side or to the stone wall on the other, unless he can with inner vision actually see the shape of the heroine's head and the length of her fingers, the slope of her neck and the folds of her gown as if she were in bodily presence before him, he cannot describe any of these things. He cannot tell what he does not know. More than that, he cannot tell to others as much as he knows; so that unless he be able to see a good deal more than he wishes to impart, he will fail to convey as much as he desires.

It is of importance to cultivate the habit of visualizing things, if one intends to describe them. The mind should be trained to conceive of them as visibly before it. This is the only way of arriving at the power of vivid portrayal. It is easy to go through the books of great writers and select those which show that the authors have this power of visualization. If a writer has it not, no skill of diction or of construction can avail to supply its lack.

In Description we have again occasion to emphasize the rule which was given in Exposition: proceed from the near to the remote; from the physical to the mental; from the obvious to the obscure. Homer, surpassed in happiness of epithet by Shakespeare only, affords abundant illustrations of this point. He says, for instance: "Wheels round, brazen, eight-spoked;" "shields smooth, beautiful, brazen, well-hammered." The particulars are given in the order in which they would naturally be observed. That the wheel is round and that the shield is smooth, the eye perceives at once. The second glance adds the fact of material, and so on.

What is meant by taking up the physical before the mental is illustrated by the following sentence from a theme picturing the appearance of a harbor in the West Indies:—

> In the distance I saw six or seven vessels in quarantine for yellow fever, all flying yellow flags.

The process of the mind is here reversed. The spectator sees the flags and reflects that they indicate quarantine for yellow fever. It is not, as a general thing, well to intersperse these mental comments. It may properly be done in a case like this, because in reading, as in seeing, the mind is likely to inquire what is the signification of the yellow flags; and it is well to answer this question in order that the reader's attention do not wander in search of an answer. If this is to be done, however, the physical appearance which gives rise to the interrogation should be given first. To reverse the order is something like giving first an answer and then the conundrum to which it belongs.

It is as bad as mixing metaphors to mingle physical and mental characteristics. In a description of the volcano of Kilauea I found this sentence:—

> The combination of vivid red and green contrasted with the deathlike quiet and grandeur of the crater.

It is not possible to contrast physical qualities like color with emotional ones such as quiet and grandeur. It is like multiplying pictures by potatoes.

Of effects used in Description the appeal to the sight is manifestly by far the most effective. Indeed, it is to be questioned whether any other is of use save in very rare instances. Of course the individual temperament of the reader has much to do with this matter, and I am perhaps influenced by the fact that while it is very easy for me to see things in imagination it is rather difficult for me to hear them. There is no question, however, that an appeal to the sense of hearing is with the average reader less likely to be convincing than that to sight. It seems to me also that the use of smell is less often successful than either of the others, and yet Kipling has shown how effective this may be if employed by a master. The mention of odors is more likely, perhaps, to belong to description by suggestion than to description simple and direct.

An important element in Description is movement. This consists in showing the details of a picture as if the mind of the reader were moving from one to another. It is secured by naming them as they would be observed; by presenting them as they would successively become apparent to some other person; or by exhibiting them in connection with their effects. Perhaps I may be able to show this by three brief pictures of a peasant girl.

1. She was a beautiful peasant girl, tall and slender, dressed in the fashion of the country, and carrying in her hand a bunch of scarlet poppies. Her snowy coif was pushed back, showing brown cheeks, a mass of black hair, and bright, startled eyes.

2. Paul watched the tall, slender peasant come up the flowery lane, twirling in her hand as she walked a handful of flaming red poppies. He was sure that she had not noticed him, and he smiled at the unconscious beauty of her brown face, clear eyes, and black, wavy hair.

3. The artist's gaze was suddenly arrested by a tall peasant girl, who walked slowly up the lane. He stopped to watch her, attracted by the grace of her slender figure, and noting appreciatively the effect against her gray gown of the scarlet poppies which she was twirling in her brown hands. As she drew nearer, and unconsciously pushed back the snowy coif, an involuntary exclamation escaped his lips at

the brilliancy of the eyes which flashed out at him from beneath her black, tumbled hair.

Such movement as there is in the first of these depends upon the arrangement of the particulars in the order in which they would naturally be perceived by the reader; in the second this order is shown to be natural by presentation of the details as if they were seen by a spectator; while in the third the effect is heightened by the introduction of the emotions aroused in the mind of the artist by the sight of the girl. Whether these examples make the fact clear or not, there is no question that the last form is the most effective. It is not always available, nor is it always appropriate; but when it is possible it is more vivid and persuasive than any other method. There is in it more suggestiveness, and hence there is more force.

As a practical example of the use of this method, this from Thomas Hardy may serve:—

How very lovable her face was to him! There was nothing ethereal about it; all was real vitality, real warmth, real incarnation. Yet when all was thought and felt that could be thought and felt about her features in general, it was her mouth which turned out to be the magnetic pole thereof. Eyes almost as deep and speaking he had seen before, and cheeks perhaps as fair; brows as arched, a chin and throat almost as shapely; her mouth he had seen nothing at all to equal on the face of the earth. To a young man with the least fire in him, that little upward lift in the middle of her top lip was distracting, infatuating, maddening. He had never before seen a woman's lips and teeth which forced upon his mind, with such persistent iteration, the old Elizabethan simile of roses filled with snow.—*Tess of the D'Urbervilles,* xxiv.

XV

Description Continued

Description by Suggestion is perhaps not to be called Description in the exact meaning of the word, but in so far as it is an attempt to call up an image it is proper to consider it so. Even if it seem but an attempt to induce in the mind the spirit of a scene, a character, or a thing, it may still be treated as Description, since the main purpose is to bring vividly to the thought of the reader the image of the thing spoken of.

It has already been said that words can add no material image to those in the mind, but must work by the rearrangement of what is already there. If I read the account of a little rustic pond I call to mind some sheet of water that I have seen. If I have lived in the South the picture is likely to be that of a lakelet bordered by moss-hung trees, while if my experiences have been confined to New England I shall involuntarily think of northern foliage and scenery. I shall in any case construct out of old images this new one. Now the mind is best able to do this for itself if simply properly aroused and guided instead of being too minutely directed. In direct description the author adds particular to particular, bidding the reader put one detail in place by the others. If a writer do this with sufficient skill, he may succeed in inducing the consciousness of the reader to follow him; but always he is leading and the other is being led. On the other hand, when a suggestion is used the reader is aroused to take, as it were, the initiative. When Dickens calls Mrs. Fezziwig "one vast, substantial smile," he stimulates the reader to picture the woman for himself. Here the imagination of the one who reads takes the lead instead of following. It goes by the path pointed out by the author, but it goes by itself. The result is that freshness and clearness of impression which belong only to what the mind does or seems to do voluntarily.

This is perhaps making more of a show of psychology than the occasion calls for or than my knowledge of that difficult science warrants; but at least it may serve to emphasize once more the fact that whatever the writer can induce the reader to do for himself is sure to be greatly more effective than anything which the writer can do for him. Herein lies the value of suggestive description. It arouses the mind to be actively receptive. Another way of putting the same thing would perhaps be to say that avowed description appeals more to the understanding, while suggestion addresses itself more directly to the imagination.

The simplest form of any description is of course the epithet. This in literal description is apt to be ineffective from its meagreness. In suggestion it is often rich and satisfactory. When Homer speaks of the "swift-footed Achilles," he has not pictured the hero, yet he conveys by the implication of the epithet an image which is not without distinctness. The same is true of such Homeric phrases as "far-darting Apollo," "laughter-loving Aphrodite," or "ox-eyed Juno." In the same way into a single simile may be condensed a description by suggestion which could be given directly only by pages. To go to the "Iliad," again, take this example:—

> As the gusts speed on, when shrill winds blow, on a day when dust lies thickest on the roads, and the winds raise together a great cloud of dust, even so their battle clashed together, and all were fain of heart to slay each other in the press with the keen bronze.—Lang's *Iliad*, xiii.

There is here no direct picture, yet the mind sees the confused and furious onslaught more clearly than if all its details were enumerated.

Lowell notes a happy instance of this sort of picturing by intimation when he says of Chaucer:

> Sometimes he describes amply by the merest hint, as where the Friar, before setting himself down, drives away the cat. We know without need of more words that he has chosen the snuggest corner.

Another remark which Lowell makes in this connection I cannot pass without quoting:—

> When Chaucer describes anything, it is commonly in one of those simple and obvious epithets or qualities that are so easy to miss. Is it a woman? He tells us that she is *fresh*; that she has *glad* eyes; that "every day her beauty newed."

Notice the phrase, "those simple and obvious epithets or qualities that are so easy to miss." Whatever we may learn later, we all begin by supposing that it is imperative for a writer to go far afield, and to discover traits, epithets, and thoughts that nobody has used before. Here as in all writing he succeeds best who most carefully confines himself to just those traits, epithets, and thoughts which people have used before, but who so uses them that they have new force. He must feel so keenly whatever he writes that his words shall seem new because of the conviction behind them; and the reader will find a continual charm in this discovery, as it were, of the meaning of familiar terms.

In common practice it is seldom that either of the two sorts of composition which I have named is used alone, and the most successful method is that which happily unites them. No literature can go far or effect much which does not call suggestion to its aid, and this is perhaps more emphatically true in Description than in any other division of composition. Description is really a kind of continued comparison of the image which is in the mind of the writer with things which the reader may be supposed to have seen. As in the use of comparison in simile, suggestion is the most effective tool at the hand of the craftsman. It might be added that the rules given for the use of figures will be found, by one who takes the trouble to examine them, to be practically and directly applicable to Description.

I have spoken carefully thus far as if Description had to do with nothing save the picturing of the physical. There was perhaps danger lest the word "picture" might seem forced if too soon applied to things mental and intangible. Description, however, has as one of its common and legitimate functions, perhaps as its highest office, the picturing of conditions of mind, of states of emotion, of all sorts of mental experiences. Its office is to call them up so vividly that the reader shall realize and share them. Not that he shall feel them as his own, but as if he saw them with the most intimate and sympathetic comprehension of them. If the reader received the sorrow of King Lear as his own, he would be in danger of going mad as King Lear went mad. If he shared as a personal experience the love of Romeo for Juliet, no other maid of actual flesh and blood would satisfy his devotion. It is not as a personal but as an imaginative experience that one is to enter into these passions. The description of an emotion is an endeavor to give a picture of it in much the same sense that a picture of a landscape is given. The reader does not in either case mistake the mental impression for the actual thing, but in both instances he is moved by the completeness and reality of the portrayal.

We come here very close to Narration, and to what has been said of the description of physical things there is not much which need be added to cover the case of immaterial things. The principles are much the same in one effort as in the other. In the bringing up of emotions and states of feeling it is more often wise to use the suggestive method. The question is moreover one of greater subtilty and delicacy. In the one case as in the other it is generally well to be governed by the order in which the details of the reality would present themselves to the inner sense. The natural is apt to be the most effective order. It is well, too, to go from the near to the remote, from the likely to the unlikely, from the simple to the complex.

It is perhaps not amiss to make here an especial point of the phrase which has been used two or three times already in other connections: Proceed generally from the physical to the mental. If without too evident artifice the physical can be made the introduction to the mental state, the impression is almost sure to be vivid. The picturing of sensations is at once the most surely effective and the most richly suggestive. Rudyard Kipling is a master of this. He constantly leads the mind of the reader to emotions through description of a physical sensation; and it is largely by his skill in this that he overcomes the difficulty of dealing with themes and emotions which are so far from the ordinary experience of an occidental audience. Stevenson is another author who understood well the use of the physical. His wonderful description of the flight through the heather in "Kidnapped" is one of the most brilliant examples of this sort of writing in modern—indeed, why should one not say in all?—literature.

In summing up, it seems to me just to say that he who would paint with words must have not only the power of writing well, but he must also possess three especial qualities. He must be able to perceive a general effect; he must be able to analyze this general effect into the details which produce it; and he must have the ability so to express these particulars that their relative values shall be preserved. The reader must first be given a broad idea of the thing, the scene, the person to be pictured. This is no less true in a case where the object is to fix the attention upon details than where the aim is to give a broad impression. The mind does not, I believe, grasp the details until after it has received the wider impression, and it is necessary to make the latter the background of the former. A remark which is made by Fuseli upon painting may be applied here. He observes that breadth is attained not by the *o*mission of details, but by their *sub*mission. While it is idle to catalogue, it is not needful to omit anything which is of use in conveying the picture sought. As long as the details are made to submit to the central thought, are kept clear and subordinate, there is no call to suppress them.

Above everything must the writer of Description see clearly what he wishes to picture, feel genuinely what he desires to communicate, and confine himself to that which is seen and felt by him,—by him alone out of all the persons who walk this earth. If it is with vague sensations that he is dealing, they must yet be clear and real to him; if it is with the emotions of imaginary persons, it is with their emotions as these are felt by him. This is the most difficult task in literary art; it is, too, when properly accomplished, the most splendid triumph of literary skill.

XVI

Narration

The more fascinating any literary work, the more difficult it is to write about it satisfactorily. The mention of the D'Artagnan Romances brings up so vivid a suggestion of life and stir, of adventure and fire, that any essay which discourses of these superb novels is almost sure to seem tame by contrast. In the mere names of "Tom Jones," "Henry Esmond," "The Scarlet Letter," there is so much potency that simply to use them as illustrations involves the danger of rendering dull and opaque by contrast the surface of exposition in which they are set like jewels. Even the specification of Narration as a division of composition connotes so many pleasant sensations that he must be a clever man who can deal with the technicalities of this sort of writing without boring his readers.

It is to be remembered, however, that before "The Lesson in Anatomy" could be painted Rembrandt had to learn how canvas is prepared and how colors are mixed; that the Ninth Symphony could not be composed until dry details of counterpoint and harmony had been mastered. It is apt to seem to the inexperienced writer as if to study the technique of art is to brush the bloom from the peach. He likes to feel that only what is spontaneous can be fresh and vital; and he forgets that in art spontaneity is impossible until the technical method has been so perfectly mastered that the creative impulse is unhampered by inability to express itself. It is not the untrained and the inexperienced who are able to be naïve and fresh in art, but only the master to whom technical excellence has become a second nature.

Having in a former talk declared Description to be the most difficult sort of composition, I am tempted now to make a bull, and to declare that Narration is more difficult still! Indeed, this would hardly be extravagant, were it not that the natural, instinctive interest of mankind in whatever is a story comes to the aid of him who writes a narrative. Narration as it exists in practice, however, is hardly to be considered alone. Of all varieties of composition, this is the one which most comprehensively embraces all other forms. It demands all the resources of the literary artist. Exposition, Argument, and Description are all enlisted in the services of the story-teller; and are so blended in the woof of his web that they can scarcely be disassociated from the narrative itself.

A succession of events can be fully told only in words. Even when we see a clever pantomime—as, for example, "L'Enfant Prodigue," which was extensively played in this country by a French company a year or two ago,—we are forced to supply in our minds a sort of running interpretation of the acts as they go on before us. Music may interpret continuous emotions, but its inadequacy to tell a definite tale is abundantly shown by that odd hybrid known as "programme music." Painting may give a succession of related themes, but between the moments chosen for representation there are gaps which break the continuity. To convey a complete and continuous account of events there is no resource in all the arts but words. It naturally follows that Narration is more intimately connected with actual life than any other sort of writing. It is the events of life which move us, and the history of these arouses the feelings as no expository or argumentative page can arouse them.

It is hardly necessary to enumerate all the many forms which Narration takes. Histories, biographies, plays, novels, romances, anecdotes, epics, stories long and stories short, the account of a journey and the folk-tale through which the fairies frisk fantastically, are all included under this division. The tedious twaddle and sea-water of "The Voyage of the Sunbeam," and the quivering pages of "Les Misérables," the account of a fire or a burglary in the morning paper, the anecdote over which a pair of drummers chuckle in a Western railway car, and the delicate romances of Hawthorne,—beautiful and pure as delicate frost-work seen by moonlight,—all these belong here, and all these are but a part. It is manifestly impossible to take up each variety separately, even were it at all worth while. We must be content to concern ourselves with general principles. Fortunately it is not difficult so to phrase these that they shall be applicable to narratives of all sorts. So many so-called stories written by inexperienced writers are merely memoranda for tales, undigested and unarranged, that there is sufficient excuse for being somewhat rudimentary in our treatment of the subject. While young authors continue to give us the material for narratives instead of properly formed and finished Narration there is at least the chance of doing good.

The first requisite in setting out to tell a story is to have a story to tell. It is true that not a few modern novels might be cited as seeming to prove the opposite of this proposition. There is a recent school of fiction in which the first principle seems to be that if one is to attempt to tell a story he must above all things else be careful not to have one in his remotest thought. The patron saint of such writers seems to be the needy knife-grinder of Canning, with his

"Story! God bless you! I have none to tell, sir."

The world in general, however, still holds logically to the old theory, and believes that to have something to relate is essential in Narration.

It is not that the theme of a narrative need be elaborate. There are many successful novels and stories with plots extremely simple. Not one of Miss Wilkins' New England idyls—those charming sublimations of the homely—has complexity or intricacy of subject. The only point is that the writer have in mind some definite and consecutive narrative, with a beginning and an end, and that he tell it as a narrative, and not as an Exposition or an Argument. The whole matter is well summed up in the phrase of Anthony Trollope: "The writer, when he sits down to commence his novel, should do so, not because he has to tell a story, but because he has a story to tell."

It would hardly do at this late day to insist, however, that the object of a story shall be simply or even primarily the narration of incident. It has been greatly the fashion during the last score of years to subordinate incident to any one of several things. Many of the greatest novelists of the present half-century have deliberately subordinated events to the study of character. There are not a few modern novels which can be adequately described only as emotional dissecting-rooms. They display the most wonderful cleverness in dismembering emotions,—too often without having a living figure or a convincing incident from one cover to the other. It is but fair to add that there are also fictions which seem to justify this method, whether we like it or not.

For our sins, moreover, the malevolent deities that deal in literary plagues have sent upon us that mongrel monstrosity, the novel with a theory. The more harmless are in the form of simpering eccentricities, or in the shape of childishly naïve whimsicalities; in the more hurtful sort authors often highly gifted lavish their powers in support of theories as generous in intention as they are mistaken and sentimental when tried by the facts upon which they are founded. We have, too, the theological novel, and the indecent novel, and more sorts than it is at all worth while to mention, in all of which the telling of a story is made the excuse for the exploiting of some view. Of these, however, we shall have occasion to speak later in connection with the moral purpose in fiction.

It has been remarked by Stevenson that in stories in which incident is made subordinate to character-drawing the interest is sure to be less vivid. He remarks:—

In character-studies the pleasure we take is critical; we watch, we approve, we smile at incongruities, we are moved to sudden heats of sympathy with courage, suffering, or virtue. But the characters are still themselves, they are not us; the more clearly they are depicted, the more widely do they stand away from us, the more imperiously do they thrust us back into our place as a spectator.... It is not character but incident that woos us out of our reserve. Something happens as we desire it to happen to ourselves; some situation, that we have long dallied with in fancy, is realized in the story with enticing and appropriate details. Then we forget the characters; then we push the hero aside; then we plunge into the tale in our own person and bathe in fresh experience; and then, and then only, do we say that we have been reading a romance.—*A Gossip on Romance.*

All these considerations are of interest to the student, and they should all be taken into account when he is looking for a subject or when he is considering methods. As a matter of practical work, it is probably true that nobody goes to work to construct stories without having some theme, some dominating suggestion in mind. He will therefore form his plot or shape his subject according to this germinating thought, without for the moment taking theories much into account. Have a theme he must, and to my thinking the more objective this is the better. The more it deals with outward things and shows what is within through them; the more it has of incident and is concerned with the actualities of life; the more it has of broad realities as distinguished from the trivialities of existence, the more likely it is to succeed.

In the treatment of a theme, the first thing is to be sure that it is thoroughly known to the writer. I do not mean that it is necessary to know every detail. I do mean that what is known should be apprehended clearly; that there should be no doubt about the end and the beginning, whatever vagueness there may be about the minutiæ of the way from one to the other. It is especially important in story-writing that the author know his characters before he write about them. It is generally safe to compose half a dozen chapters before beginning a novel, chapters which are not to be used in the book at all, but which serve to make the author acquainted with the personages he is to deal with. If every young novelist would study the methods of Hawthorne in this respect it would be to his advantage. Any one who is at all accustomed to examining literature critically knows how almost universal it is that new authors show in the first third or quarter of their books that they are slowly becoming aware of the natures of the characters in their fiction. Often the middle of the work is reached before the writer has any clear or intimate knowledge of the men and women whom he is trying to picture.

I do not believe in hard and fast rules for the construction of stories. Methods of work must vary with individual temperaments. My own way of work naturally seems to me the most logical, but I realize that this is a question which each writer must decide for himself. Personally, I find it necessary to know the general course of a story, and above all to know the end, before I can begin it. Once these are clear and true in my mind, I deliberately consider the beginning. I say "deliberately consider" because the succeeding steps have so much the air of being involuntary. Once I have decided where to begin, I devote myself to the study of my characters. I walk the streets with them; they have a share in my waking and in my sleep. I know the general course of the history I am trying to tell, but the details I am content to learn slowly. The thing which I endeavor to do is to be sure of the character of those who are involved in this history. I am not without a feeling that an old fellow who sits in solitary state in the attic of my brain tells me the incidents of the narrative, but the acquaintance of the actors I must make for myself.

Not only must a story be known to the writer but it must for the time being at least be true to him. He must believe it as he writes; he must be completely possessed by a sense of the verity of what he is telling, or he cannot persuade the reader to accept it as real. It may seem to you that this is equivalent to saying that a novelist must be a good deal like the White Queen in "Through a Looking Glass," who practiced until she was able to believe as many as six impossible things before breakfast. The difference is that the novelist does not have to practice. The characters become so vital in his mind, they act so independently and with so evident a will of their own, that it is impossible not to feel that their story is actual. Of course I do not mean that if the novelist were put on oath he would affirm that the tale is true; yet it seems to me that if I were called upon to swear that a story which I had written were not true, I should go about forever after with a humiliated sense that I had committed perjury.

I think it is the experience of every novelist that characters in a tale will often act apparently at their own good pleasure and in open defiance of the intention of the writer. They are not infrequently almost as independent of the will of the author of their being as the modern child is said to be independent of the will of the author of his. I have myself struggled to force characters to do a certain thing and have written and rewritten certain chapters in my effort to make them follow my wishes. I could set down the words which declared that they had done the thing which I desired, but I knew that I was lying and I was conscious that my characters knew that I knew it, so that of course there was nothing to do but to tear up the falsehood and tell the truth. The explanation of all this is, I suppose, that the superficial conclusions of the mind are corrected by the unconscious logic of the imagination. The characters of the personages in the story being what they are, the personages must inevitably behave in a certain way, and an underlying perception of this fundamental truth prevents an imaginative author from being able to treat his fictitious people as puppets.

The importance of knowing the end from the beginning is the same whether one is telling an anecdote or is writing a history, a romance, or a biography. It is necessary to discriminate clearly in regard to the climax of an anecdote, as it is to be sure of the climax of a novel. Everybody knows how the story which in the mouth of one man is racy and pointed becomes stupid and ineffective the moment it is told by another. I have to thank an English gentleman for having unconsciously furnished me with an example of the disadvantage of relating an anecdote with the wrong end first. He told in the smoking-room of a London hotel an incident which I dimly remembered as being in James Dodds' "Biographical Study of Chalmers," and I made a note of his version in order to compare the two. This is Dodds' story:—

[Chalmers] was present at an evening party where a very accomplished lady was discoursing most eloquent music from the fashionable opera of the day. When she was at the overture and the recitatives he looked perplexed, as if listening to a medley of madness; but when she struck upon some lively and expressive airs, he turned with a look of great relief to the gentleman who was next to him: "Do you know, sir, I love these lucid intervals!"

This is the way in which the English gentleman told it:—

"I say, don't you know, Dr. Chalmers called tunes lucid intervals. Wasn't that deuced good? Lucid intervals, by Jove! He heard a lady sing, don't you know, and that's what he said. He didn't mean all tunes of course; but she'd been playing things, you know, and putting in instrumental fal-lals and crazy things on the keys, and finally came to a song. I call that devilish witty, don't you know!"

It is hardly necessary to give examples of this fault, and this seems absurd and extravagant. It came so providentially, however, at the very time when I was writing these lectures, that it was not to be resisted.

It is excellent practice for the student to write out stories or incidents which come under his observation, and good things which he hears said or told. There are few exercises in which it is more easily possible to interest an ordinary class in composition than work of this sort, and it may be made of a good deal of value. To be really of use it is necessary that the story be told and retold until it is in the best possible form that the student can compass. It should be done as carefully as if it were a great and complete narrative.

I said in another talk that I am not willing to concede that conversation is an art which comes by nature, and the justice of this must be especially felt by one who listens when story-telling is the order of the day. Those who succeed in telling a story well are those who have taken the trouble to learn how. It is a mistake to suppose that the carelessly spoken anecdote which is so felicitously put that it seems to be the thought of the moment has cost the narrator nothing. He has consciously labored to attain the art of telling things well; and while here as everywhere natural gifts count, the man who cultivates a small talent can generally outshine him who leaves a great talent to take care of itself.

I have perhaps spoken so as to give the impression that a story makes itself. I mean nothing of the sort. It is true that the first germ of a fiction is often caught in the mind as a plumy-winged seed of the wild clematis is caught in the cranny of a wall. Sometimes a chance word, the sight of a face in the crowd, a bit of information or talk, will become the suggestion from which a story will grow. It must be nurtured, however, if its growth is to be vigorous or symmetrical. It must be brooded over and watched; it must be nourished and tended. When a story is well formed in the mind and the characters are well defined, it will grow and develop spontaneously, but it must be given a good start first. In other words, the theme must be dwelt upon until it is so completely a part of the thought that the mind will carry it forward unconsciously, and the tale will seem to be going on of itself.

It is customary to say that all narrative has four elements: first, what happened,—the plot or story; second, what persons were concerned,—the characters; third, the situation, which is both in time and space,—in other words the when and the where; fourth, the central motive,—the thing of interest or significance for which the whole is told. These elements seem to me to be likely to come to the writer in the order in which I have named them. Sometimes he is aware of the central purpose first, especially in fiction written with a declared motive; but this does not appear to be the natural order in the case of fiction really imaginative. An author must of course have a comprehension of the central motive before he begins to write, but he deduces it from his plot rather than forms a plot to embody the idea. All this analysis is of more value in revision of work or in criticism than in actual composition. The writer who is really alive and interested in what he is doing thinks of his story as a story and as a transcript from life, not as a combination of four elements.

In this same line of criticism and revision it is well to note that Narration is necessarily specific, progressive, and cumulative. It is specific in that it deals with facts rather than with theories, with incidents rather than with deductions, with events rather than with reflections. It is progressive in that the interest must move forward, and the theme must advance with the incidents. A collection of incidents does not make a narrative any more than a pile of lumber makes a house. There must be a sequence of events related to each other by the tie of cause and effect. Narration is cumulative because this chain of cause and effect must lead to some conclusion, some climax, some end. Even in the relation of the most trifling anecdotes these three qualities are to be found, and in their perfection lies the secret of the greatest works of literature. The theorists who excuse inartistic and unsymmetrical fiction by the theory that a novel should be a piece cut out of life and having neither beginning or end, forget that that which is comely and fit, so long as it is part of the living tree-trunk, becomes an unsightly block when it is chopped out. It must be shaped and finished to be again beautiful. The story which has by relation been taken from its place in actual life must be worked and polished by art; it must become a whole in itself or it is forever an uncomely log, crudely disfiguring the landscape and fit only to be used as material for work or to feed the fire.

XVII

Narration Continued

The point of view is of no less importance in Narration than in Description. It is perhaps not so strictly observed, because to the ordinary writer it is less obvious. As a rule it is not specifically announced. If a tale is in the form of an autobiography, as "Robinson Crusoe," for instance, or "Henry Esmond," the point of view is of course that of the perceptions of the character who relates. To this the author must confine himself, and every time that he introduces incidents, words, or thoughts which this character could not have known he violates it. He breaks the continuity and interrupts the impression of the reader. Less obviously, many novelists practically hold to the personality of one or two of their characters for their point of view. Without any specification of the fact, they refrain from telling anything which might not have been known or felt by these personages. An admirable illustration of this method is "The Scarlet Letter." Throughout the entire book there are practically only three individualities through whose perceptions the reader is called upon to look. The author does not claim at any point to be confining himself to these or to any one of these; yet the comments and reflections which are]outside the observation of Hester Prynne, Arthur Dimmesdale, and Roger Chillingworth are so close to them as almost to seem part of their thought. What is not actually within their perception is little more than the author's expression of their unformulated emotions or interpretations of their motives. More than two thirds of the book is given from the standpoint of the inner life of the wearer of the scarlet letter, and the greater portion of the remainder is from that of the minister.

Of course the writer may, if he choose, take as the point of view the position of all knowledge. He may decide to speak as one who knows every thought. The inexperienced writer is especially likely to be fond of this method. He is apt to dance about in a confused and confusing will-o'-the-wisp ubiquity. The early days of story-writing are marked by a delightful sense of omnipotence and omniscience which seldom outlives the completion of the first novel. While this feeling lasts the author holds it a sort of duty to allow his readers to look in turn through the eyes of each of his characters. It is as if he were proprietor of a peep-show. He cannot bring himself to defraud the reader by putting him off with anything less than a glimpse through every peep-hole. Whatever is the point of view chosen, it must, as in all other sorts of composition, be held throughout. The point of view of a single character is that which gives most intensity to a tale. The character chosen becomes the embodiment of the thoughts and emotions of the reader for the time being, and dominates all others. This is perhaps even more emphatically true when this is done by implication. The assumption of a single personality in the story as that which shall dominate seems to come from the absorbing interest of the author in this character, and it almost surely not only makes this the most significant figure in the tale, but imparts to the story fervor and strenuousness.

It is perhaps well to add a word of warning. It is not wise to expect too much from the reader in the way of coming to a point of view remote from his ordinary attitude of mind. The short stories of Miss Wilkins tacitly ask the reader to assume the mood of an observer who sees the pathetic and yet humorous quality in homely life. They owe their success in no small degree to the simplicity of this point of view and the consistency with which it is kept throughout. In "Pembroke" the same author goes farther, and tacitly asks us to regard the quarrels of obstinate and ill-tempered rustics with the profound seriousness demanded by the crushing blows of inexorable fate. It is asking too much. We cannot look upon these rural contests of obstinacy with the solemnity demanded by a Greek tragedy. It is a far cry from the

"Œdipus" or the "Antigone" to "Pembroke;" and Miss Wilkins makes too great a demand upon the reader when she seems to assume so profound a solemnity. It seems to me that herein lies one secret of the disappointment felt in reading "Pembroke" after the delights of the author's short stories.

The selection of incidents is naturally a matter of the greatest importance in the construction of any narrative, whether historic or fictitious. It is evident that it is impossible to tell the whole truth about any person, whether it be a character real in flesh and blood or one of the personages so much more real in imagination. A novelist cannot set down all the particulars of the life of those about whom he writes, and in the case of any story it must be only the significant incidents that will attract the reader. The literary code which professes to find all facts of life of equal value is on the face of it absurd, and had the men who claim to hold it lived up to their creed their novels would never have got beyond manuscript. Choice is necessary, and the great principle of choice is significance.

When we speak of significance, we of course mean the relation of the incident to the central motive of the narrative. The rule is that details are to be introduced or omitted as they do or do not form an essential part of the whole. If the writer have not the art so to weave in his most interesting and novel incident that it shall be an integral portion of the web, he must omit it. The taste of our time has very little patience with that excrescence which used to be known as an episode. Whatever is told should help forward the general plan of the work. The space and the importance given to each portion must manifestly be determined by its value in the entire scheme. Proportion is in effect the same here as in any other form of composition, a matter which depends upon the intention of the whole.

The young writer who is moved to delight a waiting and to his fancy impatient world with a new work of fiction has generally read a good many stories, and is likely to have gained from them some unconscious sense of proportion. This may save him from utter failure, but he is likely to stumble over two serious obstacles. In the first place he is sure to have his favorite situations, and is apt to linger over these in a fond belief that his readers will be as charmed as he is with these portions of his tale. In the second place, he is likely to feel a certain security in using incidents which are taken from real life.

Of the first of these it is sufficient to say that such is the perversity of fate that it almost never happens that the reader agrees with the writer—especially with the untrained writer—in regard to the most interesting portions of a book. Indeed, it is not amiss for a writer to be a little suspicious of the parts of his work which he regards with most favor. It is of importance to cultivate a dispassionate habit of mind, and always to judge the value of portions with relation to the whole rather than with reference to the author's likes or dislikes.

The second point is one which needs to be emphasized. The moment a man begins to write, his friends begin to offer true stories for use,— not one out of a hundred being usable; and they invariably commend these subjects by saying that they are things which really happened. It is impossible to make the general public understand that the fact that a thing happened is rather more likely to be against it as literary material than in its favor. Facts are admirable from their suggestiveness. No fiction is of value which is not founded upon them. They are to be used, however, as material which must be shaped and moulded before it can be used. They are the rocks from the quarry that must be dressed before they are fit building material. The danger lies in accepting actuality instead of literary propriety as the measure of value. There is perhaps no rule more useful or more necessary to young writers of fiction than to beware of the truth. If in a first novel are found scenes and incidents which are unreal and extravagant, the chances are that these are the things which have been confidently taken from real life,—and which have become hopelessly unreal in the transfer. In Narration as in Description the thing sought is not the truth but the impression of truth. The question is not whether what is told is true, but whether it seem true. We all know extraordinary incidents which are real yet which are too improbable to be used in fiction. The reason is obvious.

It is necessary for fiction to be probable, while truth is free from all restrictions. The novelist is never allowed to take refuge behind the fact that a thing is veracious. He may tell whatever he has the art to make appear true, but the criterion of his success is the semblance of verity rather than verity itself. Aristotle formulated all this long ago,—"Prefer an impossibility which seems probable to a probability which seems impossible." The philosophy of the matter is that fiction is tried by truth to the laws which lie behind fact, and that it is no less true in being false than reality is in being true.

It is to be remembered, however, that probability is largely a matter of consistency. There is always an implied hypothesis, a certain set of conditions tacitly agreed to, by which the truth, or rather the apparent truth, of any narrative is to be tried. If one is writing history, the hypothesis calls for actual facts and things which really occurred; if it is a novel which is in construction, actuality is no longer demanded, but probability according to the time and place is essential; an author may go farther by writing avowed romance, and may put events impossible and improbable into the very midst of the life of to-day, if he will but keep them consistent throughout. It is a question of what the writer attempts to do. If he choose frankly to cut loose from fact and write a fairy story, the hypothesis gives his fancy range, and here it is the strict truth which must be shunned as a violation of the implied conditions. In a number of folk tales we read passages like this:—

> Then the fox stretched out his tail, the king's son seated himself upon it, and away they went over stock and stone, so that the wind whistled through their hair.

It would be manifestly a violation of the rules of fairy lore to say instead:—

> Then the fox stretched out his tail, and the king's son tried to seat himself upon it; but of course it would not support him, so he rolled over in the mud.

To thrust facts upon the reader here is to depart from the standard. When we sit down to read fairy tales we have tacitly consented to believe the impossible, and upon this assumption fairy lore becomes, in the happy phrase of Douglas Jerrold, "as true as sunbeams."

All this, however, is the exception, and as it is an exception which is sufficiently obvious, it is enough to mention it. The general rule for Narration is: In writing history select details with reference to their significance and their truth; in fiction with reference to their significance and their probability. In every case, significance is an essential quality. It is so easy to confound minuteness with subtlety; to suppose that to be finical is to be true; to assume that to be exact is to be effective; that more than one gifted author has come to grief and has wasted his powers through these errors. The measure of subtlety, of truth, and of effectiveness, is the relative value as measured by the central idea of the composition.

The order of events in a narrative depends chiefly upon the principle of cause and effect. Since every cause produces its effect, it follows that the sequence of incidents will generally be practically chronological. Where there are a number of threads involved and the plot is complicated, a good deal of ingenuity is often required to keep things clear, and to secure at the same time a continuous progression in the narrative. This is a problem with which the historian has almost always to deal, and upon his cleverness in solving it depends much of his success. The only rule to be given is that the writer shall have a careful and definite plan. In a simple tale it is often possible to depend upon the knowledge of the end to be reached, and to trust to one's instinct for the rest. With an intricate theme this will not do. If one is driving a mild-mannered horse in a light wagon, it is usually enough to know the general direction, since it is possible from time to time to stop to inquire the way; in running a complicated system of railway trains the same method would be madness.

One matter involved in this question of the order of incidents is that of where and how a story shall begin. Often it is wise to commence with a striking incident or situation, and it is rare that a story can be effectively begun without there being more or less which must be told of what has gone before the actual tale. Much care is needed in managing this. It is one of the simplest devices, and it remains one of the most effective which have been devised, to have all explanations of this sort made to some personage in the tale instead of to the reader directly. If a story start with the striking appearance of the hero in some extraordinary situation, it is much more effective and pleasing to have the spectators, those who in the narrative are represented as seeing him, ask and obtain information in regard to his past and to the events which brought him to this place or situation, than it is for the author in a deliberate manner to set out to inform the reader.

Never presume on the reader's patience and indulgence. The "gentle reader" of old-fashioned literature does not exist now, if indeed he ever existed. The modern reader is far more ready to be bored than to be interested, and all devices for persuading and holding his attention must be carefully attended to.

Of essential importance in story-telling is movement. This is an advantage in other forms of composition, but indispensable in Narration. There can be no sense of unity, no continuity of interest, unless there is a constant sense of progression. A story can no more stand still than can life. When the incidents cease to carry the reader forward, it is as if the heart stopped beating. Each incident in a narrative, as in existence, must stand in relation to what comes before it of effect to cause, and to what follows it of cause to effect. It is necessary to make the reader feel that he is ever going forward, now slowly and now swiftly, according to the exigencies of the tale. Contrast, variety, relative importance, have all to be considered. When the reader is eager to reach some culmination, when he is excited in regard to some crisis in the narrative, it is often wise to condense days into a sentence, hours into a phrase. Again, there are times when it is important to prepare the mind for a situation, to go slowly in order that an effect be produced by the cumulative force of trifles. No hard-and-fast rule can be given to govern this progression. The technical means by which swiftness or deliberation are secured are simple and easily learned. The whole matter is pretty well covered by the statement that many words and minute details retard movement, while few words and a suppression of particulars give rapidity. When to employ these means the writer must learn from the study of the work of the masters, from the careful consideration of what result he wishes to insure, and above all by a close examination of the manner in which effects are produced in real life. Naturally, the movement is swifter as the tale nears its conclusion, and in passages which deal with exciting and intense emotions. Illustrations are hardly possible in limited space, but the climax of any masterpiece may serve as an example.

Description and dialogue must be subordinate to the movement of a story, as they must be subordinate to the general purpose. Speaking broadly, dialogue aids swiftness of progression, and description delays it; yet an over-abundance of talk may retard as effectually as profuse word-painting. With dialogue we shall have to do later, and here it is enough to say that talk which really belongs to the tale, which helps the story forward, adds sprightliness to the movement. We all know how the elder Dumas makes dialogue increase the vivacity and the rapidity of movement of his dashing romances. What can be told in the speech of the characters in a narrative seems generally to go forward with more briskness than what is related in the words of the author.

The mention of Description brings us to the scene of a narrative. The setting of a tale is not unlike the mounting of a play. When the use of nature in fiction was fresher than now the affair was very simple. It was only necessary to bring in gloomy skies and wailing winds as accompaniments for a doleful situation, or to have the flowers, the sunshine, and the birds properly specified when things were going happily. The birds sang most obligingly for the old novelists, utterly ignoring the habits which ornithologists had with painful care observed,—they warbled when they were wanted, although they were called upon at times of day when they had never before dreamed of piping up:—

Singing gladly all the moontide,Never waiting for the noontide.

In less artistic fiction there is still something of this method. There are many transiently popular novels where in the closing chapter the autumn rain still falls dismally upon a lonely grave, or the summer sun—the June sun—and the obliging dicky-birds decorate the wedding of the long-persecuted but at last triumphant heroine, transcendently lovely in white satin.

In really serious work the matter has become more intricate. Nature must be used without the appearance of design. It is recognized that no man can command the weather, and the trick of seeming to manage the elements is no longer tolerated. Art must conceal art. Even contrasts have been used until it is necessary to be very cautious in employing them. The villains no longer steal through smiling gardens whose snowy lilies, all abloom, and sending up perfume like incense from censers of silver, seem to rebuke the wicked. The thing sought now is the appearance of naturalness. Simplicity and directness are the prime qualities to be kept in mind. Set a story carefully, but above all things be sure that it does not appear that pains have been taken. The finest art is that which works with apparent frankness, seeming to display its methods without disguise, yet in reality producing its effects by a skill which is utterly beyond perception.

One of the faults most common with beginners is self-consciousness. The inexperienced writer is apt to show that he is not sure how what he writes will be received. Cultivate the attitude of being conscious of nothing but the story to be told. Above all, do not seem to apologize. In fiction as elsewhere apologies are apt to breed contempt. The writer who seems to plead to be excused inevitably suggests that there is need of excuse. Tell a story or leave it, but never take the middle course of telling it with apologies, direct or indirect. Often the self-conscious author shows that he secretly fears that he will be thought to lack cleverness if he allows himself so to be imposed upon by his characters as to think them real. If they are not real to him he should not be telling their history. The slightest appearance of doubt on his part ruins all illusion and the story along with it.

On the other hand, it is a mistake to expect the reader to share an emotion simply from being told that it is felt by the writer. Every phrase like "I felt," "I was amused," "I was enraged," and so on, which is not amply supported by the narrative, weakens the effect. It is generally enough to destroy the entire flavor of any ordinary witticism to tell the reader that it is droll. It sometimes will do to say that the characters of the tale thought a thing funny, but even this is a somewhat dangerous expedient. If a thing does not strike the reader as amusing, it is of little use to inform him that it is his duty to find it so. An author has no business to put himself in the attitude of a verger who leads pilgrims from one historic spot to another, saying in effect at each, "Here it is necessary that you feel yourselves thrilled!"

When everything else has been said, the essential thing in regard to Narration is that it shall be interesting. It is the old question of Force. "Tediousness," observes Dr. Johnson, with his usual sententiousness, "is the most fatal of faults." He might have added that it is a fault so serious that it overcomes all excellences. Macaulay inquires, "Where lies the secret of being amusing? and how is it that art, eloquence, and diligence may all be employed in making a book dull?" Dullness is less easily forgiven in narrative than in any other form of composition. The avowed aim of a story is to entertain; and if it fail of this, its merits count for nothing. The specific methods by which interest may be secured or increased must be studied with the realization that the very existence of narrative depends upon them.

The first point is to be interested one's self. In other words, the first great secret is earnestness.

The second is closely allied to it. It is to be perfectly straightforward. This secret is sincerity.

The first of these calls for the telling of a thing as if the writer really cares for it, as if it is something which seems to him richly worth relating; while the second insists that he shall treat his readers with every appearance of frankness. He shall appear to conceal nothing which it is for the interest of the tale for him to tell, and he shall try to take no advantage by telling that of which he is not himself completely persuaded, nothing which does not seem to him a vital portion of the history, real or fictitious, which he set out to relate. Hawthorne, when asked the secret of his style, said: "It is the desire to tell the simple truth as honestly and as vividly as one can." Many entire books on rhetoric have less wisdom in them than is in this single sentence.

Making a somewhat different division of the subject, we may say that interest in Narration comes from three sources: the plot, the incident, and the development of character. The story which depends upon plot alone goes by quickly. Only while it has novelty can it command attention, and it is scarcely to be read a second time. The tale which depends upon incident alone—if there be such—would be not unlike a book of anecdotes, too fragmentary to be effective as a whole. That in which the drawing of character is the chief feature is likely to be heavy and sure to be restricted to a limited audience. In the masterpiece, plot, incident, and character-drawing are combined. The great novelists have never essentially varied in their methods, and in the work of Cervantes, Fielding, Thackeray, Hawthorne, and the rest, style, character, and story are all integral parts of the whole.

It is perhaps not amiss to say here a word in regard to the collection of material and to what is meant by the study of nature. I have already repeated the truism that the writer must ever be on the alert for material. If he is to write stories he is to undertake the reproduction of human life, and it is above all needful that he understand human life. He cannot be too careful in his consideration of the world about him. He must be constantly examining the acts of his fellow men; constantly saying to himself: "What were the motives which led to that act? What were the feelings aroused by that experience? What the emotions in such a situation?" He must make his own inner experience the test, and from the less divine the greater. He may to a great extent judge the motives which actuate men and women in important crises from those which have moved him in circumstances seemingly trivial. A well-known New England story-teller said to me once when I praised a tale in which she had shown most vividly the remorse of a man who had committed a great crime: "It will amuse you to hear how I knew what that man's feelings were. Once when I was a child I burned up my sister's doll in a fit of anger. The remorse I suffered over that foolish performance was the material that I made my story out of." There is a good illustration of the way in which the creative mind works. From the nature of its own emotions it is able to appreciate the feelings of others, and to see that in feeling there is more question of degree than of kind. His own being is the only one into which a writer can really look. What he finds in his own heart is the key by which to read the cipher which is written in the hearts of others.

Narration is the form of literature which most universally appeals to men, and it is no less that form which most affects human conduct. Men who could not be brought to give ear to a sermon may be taught by a parable or moved by a tale. It is in narrative that prose rises most surely and indisputably to the rank of a fine art, so that while the masterpieces of fiction remain it will be impossible to question the right of prose literature to claim a place beside painting, sculpture, music, and poetry. Art is the regenerator of the world, and in modern times it is in the form of fiction that it most easily and most widely reaches the hearts of men.

XVIII

Accessories of Narration

The range of Narration is so wide that it is well to look a little more carefully at the means of producing effects in this especial department of composition. The subject is at once so fascinating and so complicated that it would not be difficult to make an entire course of lectures upon it, although in the end we might be brought to the humiliating consciousness that no amount of lecturing could make novelists of us. In the limits of these talks it is impossible to do more than to consider briefly the more important matters which occupy the attention of the story-teller; and those which first come to mind are the things which it is customary to name Local Color, Dialect, Dialogue, Character Drawing, and Moral Purpose.

Local color in the modern sense was invented in the present century. It is true that the writers of other times had employed the same device before, but it has been consciously sought and has been supplied with this name within recent times. It might be asked by a cynic why the quality is any better now that it is ticketed and talked about in reviews than it was in the days of Theocritus and Kalidasa and Boccaccio; but so many things have been used before modern generations were thought of that if we are not to have the privilege of regarding things as new when they have been newly named we are likely to be at a desperate loss for novelty.

By local color is now meant the bringing out of the peculiarities of the locality where the scene of a tale is laid. It is evident that there is no spot so poor as not to have characteristics which distinguish it from all others. It is the aim of many modern story-tellers to give this especial local flavor with the most faithful and often painful vividness.

Indeed, there are not a few recent stories which seem to exist for no other reason than to exploit the accidental qualities of remote and hitherto undescribed places.

This is an age in which competition between periodicals has waxed warm, and to the desire of editors to procure novelties is largely due the increase of the already rather tiresomely abundant examples of local color and of dialect. An air of freshness may be imparted to a tale by laying the scene in places practically unknown in fiction. Accidents of custom and manners arrest the attention for the moment, and it is due to this fact that the great mass of stories marked by this peculiarity have succeeded. The principle is not unlike that of drawing a crowd to the theatre by new scenery. A tale which is really vital can do without local color, as a really strong play succeeds without elaborate setting.

This is not, however, the whole of the matter. A good play may be helped by novel effects of scenery and a tale good in itself may be improved by local color. Detailed description of local peculiarities may make more clear to the reader the character and the motives of the personages in a narrative. All men are influenced by their surroundings, and to be familiar with unusual social conditions is often essential to the understanding of acts or opinions which have been done or held under them. To make intelligible the story of Hester Prynne and Arthur Dimmesdale, Hawthorne was obliged to set forth something of the manners and morals of colonial days. Scott could not have made comprehendable the tale of Rob Roy without giving some idea of what life in the Highlands was like in the time of that redoubtable chieftain. The author must in any case impart to the reader whatever special information is necessary to the best effect of his fiction.

The comment which it seems fair to make in this connection is that here is to be applied the rule which should govern the management of all details in narration,—namely, that everything shall be kept subordinate to the central purpose of the work. So long as particular description aids in bringing out more clearly the main idea of the whole, so long as it is used as a means and not as an end, so long as the setting is kept subordinate to the story, so long it is good. The moment what is called local color is allowed to dominate a story, it must injure the permanent effect. The literary mechanic who is writing stories simply to sell them will usually find it easy to dispose of studies of local peculiarities which are piquant, whether they are true or not. There is nothing to object to in this, but this work is not to be confounded with legitimate Narration, and it is not to be looked upon as permanent literature. Local color is accidental rather than essential. It depends upon circumstances which belong to a place rather than to human nature. It follows that it is not in itself of permanent interest, and that work depending upon it for interest must go by as soon as the novelty is passed. The work of Miss Wilkins, Miss Jewett, Miss Brown, and the rest, has attracted attention through the fidelity with which it presented peculiarities of New England rural life. The claim to permanent value in each, however, rests on other and higher grounds. In so far as they are true to the fundamental and essential characteristics of humanity, in so far as they deal with the constant emotions of men and women as men and women, and not as eccentric types evolved by peculiarities and environment, they have permanent value—and no farther.

Closely allied with local color, and indeed in many cases hardly to be distinguished from it, is dialect. We are all familiar with a certain strange appearance which has of late years come over the pages of the magazines, a sort of epidemic of which the most prominent characteristics are the misspelling of words and a plentiful spattering of apostrophes, as if the secret of literary art lay in eccentric and intermittent orthography. We have been instructed that these startling productions were dialect stories, and whether we have professed to like them or not has depended largely upon our daring to say what we thought. There are, it is true, dialect stories which we must all admire and enjoy,—many of them in spite of their strange language rather than because of it,—but none the less is the multiplicity of tales in dialect a visitation not unlike the Egyptian plague of swarming flies or of sprawling frogs.

The object of the use of dialect is of course to produce what might be called a personal local color. To personages who belong to nationalities other than his own a writer often gives phrases in their own tongue or conforming to the idiom of their own language in order to convey a lively impression of their being foreigners. To produce a vivid sense of the fact that his characters are Creoles of New Orleans and to suggest all the romantic flavor of life among them, George Cable used dialect in that delightful book, "Old Creole Days;" to make the reader realize the especial local and race peculiarities of one character or another Thomas Nelson Page used one negro dialect in "Marse Chan" and Joel Chandler Harris another in "Uncle Remus." In these and similar cases the dialect used is really, as far as the general reader is concerned, an unknown tongue. Its correctness or incorrectness cannot be judged by the general public to which these tales are addressed, and its use must therefore be flavor rather than accuracy, impression rather than information, picturesqueness rather than literalness.

The proper use of dialect is often a great aid in characterization. Some figures it is all but impossible to individualize without this means. There are figures in Scott which would not be at all the same thing if stripped of their dialect; while in each of the stories mentioned above there are instances of the same thing. It is to be remembered, however, that this is a subsidiary purpose. In other words it is a detail of fiction. Dialect is written for the sake of the story, and woe to that author who produces a story for the sake of a dialect. The tales of the "Soldiers Three," the "Window in Thrums," "Old Creole Days," succeed for other qualities than the dialect, and the dialect is good because it helps to make effective something better. It is even not improbable that with a large body of readers these and kindred books succeed only in spite of their dialect, since even at its best this perversion of language is apt to be in itself somewhat irritating even if not perplexing.

Actually to reproduce a dialect as it is spoken is a feat so difficult that it is worse than idle to attempt it outside of works on philology. Dialectic peculiarities are always largely matters of accent, of voice quality, and of inflection. The sounds of vowels and consonants may be indicated, but it is all but impossible to set down the rising and falling of the voice which is the most characteristic quality of these forms of speech. Printed words cannot reproduce that species of intoning which has so large a share in making unintelligible to foreigners the speech of London cabmen and porters. Indeed, it is to be doubted whether any written dialect is to be regarded as a very exact reproduction of the genuine thing,—a statement which would probably be regarded with contemptuous anger by the devotees of the dialect story, if any still survive. Certainly it is true that dialect does not have to be genuine to be successful. The dialect of the "Biglow Papers" was never spoken on the face of the earth. It is none the worse for that, so far as I can see. It has the effect for which it was intended, and nothing more could reasonably be asked. Mr. Lowell made it with the most careful patience, and apparently believed in it with beautiful faith. He set nothing down, or rather he tried to set nothing down, which he had not heard from the lips of Yankee rustics; but in the first place no one man ever used all those distorted words and phrases, belonging sometimes to different localities; and in the second, letters cannot reproduce the peculiar sounds and accents of rural New England. Yet this dialect has imposed for a quarter of a century upon no inconsiderable portion of the American reading public, and it will probably continue to impose upon English readers until the end of time.

The inability of readers to judge of the accuracy of dialect is inseparable from its use. How many are acquainted with the vernacular of "Thrums," the patois of New Orleans Creoles, the dialect of Mexican mining camps, or the speech of the half-breeds of Canada or the West Indian islands? No danger that the general reader will measure work by reality obliges the writer of dialect to be accurate. The only restraining influence is the difficulty of making a manufactured dialect consistent and convincing. The story-teller studies dialect as it is spoken, not for the sake of being right, but because this is the surest way to obtain the appearance of being right. The only essential thing is to be convincing.

The danger in the use of dialect is not far to seek. Its literary value is that of flavor. As long as this fact is recognized it may properly be employed. The difficulty is that the great and inglorious company of imitators have written dialect for its own sake,—or perhaps for their own sake!—and thereby not only have produced things dreadful to contemplate, but have so wearied the soul of readers that it has become dangerous to use it legitimately. Dialect in literature is a condiment and not a viand; it is mustard and not beef; it is never to be employed for its own sake any more than are commas and capitals, paragraphs and periods. Almost every inexperienced writer who tries his hand at dialect—and most experienced ones—will overdo it. The French, with their instinctive literary sense, may well be studied in this connection. They understand that the value of patois is its suggestiveness, and they go in its use just so far as is necessary to impart the flavor required, and there they stop. This is the legitimate method. I have nothing to say of those disfigurements which appear in some of the periodicals, sketches which are written for the sake of exhibiting a special dialect. They do not come under the head of literature except in the sense in which the word includes the dictionary and thesaurus. They may be of interest to the student of philology, but they cannot concern the imaginative reader.

The best quality which dialect can give is an impression of individuality, of quaintness or remoteness from conventional and hackneyed experiences. It must be written with care and sobriety. The writer must remember that the day is definitely past when it was possible to produce effects simply by misspelling. It is well to keep in mind also that even the ability to write a dialect never so perfectly is not necessarily a reason for using it. The employment of local forms of language, like local color, must be subordinate to the purposes of the story. It is always a means and never legitimately an end. It is, moreover, a good deal discredited by over-use and abuse, so that it must be employed with double caution.

One more word of warning it seems well to add. The employment of dialect and of local color as a means of producing literary effect is apt to impart to work a transient character. Their effect is less likely to be permanently pleasing than that of almost any other thing legitimately among the resources of the story-teller. The principle that it is well to appeal to ordinary experiences and to ordinary tastes comes in here. The general reader soon tires of dialect unless it be very simple and is supported by all other devices within the range of art. To write dialect is likely to be at best to sacrifice permanent to temporary success. The greatest writers have usually employed it sparingly. Shakespeare almost never resorted to it; Fielding scarcely used it at all; Scott tried it much more largely, but the Scotch speech was all but universal among his people, and it has certainly been oftener a hindrance than a help to his continued success; Thackeray put little of it into his best work; Hawthorne passed it by; and even Dickens depended upon it very little, despite the temptations which his characters constantly offered. Thomas Hardy has given us the best rustics since Shakespeare with not much more than an indication of dialect. I do not wish to insist upon the point too strongly, but the principle seems to me a sound one, and it is certainly worth the consideration of any student of the art of writing fiction.

The art of writing dialogue is by no means the least difficult thing which the story-teller has to learn, and there are very many who are not able to acquire it to the end of their days. If a rule could be devised by which good and pleasing dialogue could be written, it would go far toward making it possible for every man to be his own novelist. To give to the talk of a tale the air of naturalness and ease, to make it take its place in the story and be attractive without being too clever or too formal, to give it character and consistency, to impart to it movement and vivacity, to be sure that it helps forward the narrative in which it is set,—all these difficulties must be overcome before an author can be said to write good dialogue.

The first essential in dialogue is naturalness. Some authors get on without this, but they get on in spite of lacking it and are constantly hampered by the lack. The most striking instance of this in modern fiction is probably George Meredith, a novelist who makes his way with more encumbrances than any other living man of genius. Take, for instance, this bit, chosen almost at random:—

"Have you walked far to-day?"

"Nine and a half hours. My Flibbertigibbet is too much for me at times, and I had to walk off my temper." ...

"All those hours were required?"

"Not quite so long."

"You are training for your alpine tour."

"It's doubtful whether I shall get to the Alps this year. I leave the Hall, and shall probably be in London with a pen to sell."

"Willoughby knows that you leave him?"

"As much as Mont Blanc knows that he is going to be climbed by a party below. He sees a speck or two in the valley."

"He has spoken of it."

"He would attribute it to changes."

—*The Egotist*, viii.

This does as a matter of fact somewhat help forward the story from which it is taken, but could anybody get from it the idea that two living beings were talking together?

The great principle of the impression of truth instead of a servile imitation of truth is the secret of good talk in fiction. It is necessary to keep clear on the one hand of formality and stiffness, and on the other of stupid closeness in mere imitation. In actual talk there are inaccuracies, broken sentences, phrases of which the meaning is evident from some glance or gesture, repetitions and careless constructions, all of which would lose their force or gain undue importance if set down in print. To preserve or too closely to imitate these characteristics of genuine conversation is to give an impression of unreality, or commonplaceness and even of vulgarity. The rambling speech is often pleasantly and appropriately imitated. The inimitable Nurse in "Romeo and Juliet" stands at the head of talkers of this sort, but there are excellent specimens in the fiction of our own century. Miss Austen possessed the secret of this futile volubility to perfection, and Mrs. Stowe's best literary work is her management of the discursive talk of Sam Lawson.

That conversation should be in keeping with the characters speaking is one of those things so obvious that it is unsafe to leave them unsaid. It is another application of the principle of the point of view. The natural tendency of the beginner is to put into the mouths of his personages not what they would say but what he would have them say. If he sufficiently realize them in his own mind there will be little danger of this. The remedy is to know his characters. The people in any book will talk consistently if they are real to the author. They will say what they wish to say and not what he wishes them to say, and that is the whole secret.

Most young writers compose pages of dialogue which seems to them clever, which, when it is written, they read over with tender admiration, generally not without a little amazement that they have done so well and a conviction that this at least imparts distinction to their book,—when as a matter of fact the whole thing is simply an amateurish mistake. It is one of the many pitfalls which egotism and inexperience dig for the unwary writer, who forgets that success can be achieved only when the end of a work is the work and not the worker. The elaborator of his own opinions into the form of talk is not writing dialogue; he is but making a weak concession to his individual vanity. His punishment is that he cannot deceive the public. Readers may not know their right hands from their left, but they know when they are bored, and they are always bored when the progress of the tale is interrupted to afford an author opportunity to display himself.

Anthony Trollope puts this matter well in his "Autobiography:"—

There is no portion of a novelist's work in which this fault of episodes is so common as in dialogue. It is so easy to make two persons talk on any casual subject with which the writer presumes himself to be conversant! Literature, philosophy, politics, or sport may be handled in a loosely discursive style; and the writer, while indulging himself, is apt to think he is pleasing the reader. I think he can make no greater mistake. The dialogue is generally the most agreeable part of a novel; but it is only so as long as it tends in some way to the telling of the main story. It need not seem to be confined to this, but it should always have a tendency in this direction. The unconscious critical acumen of a reader is both just and severe. When a long dialogue on extraneous matter reaches his mind, he at once feels that he is being cheated into taking something that he did not bargain to accept when he took up that novel. He does not at that moment require politics or philosophy, but he wants a story. He will not, perhaps, be able to say in so many words that at some certain point the dialogue has deviated from the story; but when it does he will feel it.—Ch. xii.

Of course the matter is made more complicated by the fact that it is often the office of dialogue to indicate character rather than action. How far the writer may introduce talk simply to illustrate mental characteristics or moods is a thing to be decided by each writer for himself and learned by observation. It is not amiss for a young writer to consider carefully how far he is himself able to enjoy this in the work of others; and in any case he must learn to distinguish between what is written genuinely to illustrate mental traits and that which is really put in simply to show his own cleverness.

There are two points in the writing out of dialogue which it is well to keep in mind: first that care must be taken never to leave the reader in doubt who is speaking, and second that interspersed comments be used with skillful nicety.

In a conversation which consists of a somewhat extended succession of short speeches it is often hard for the reader to keep in mind without effort who say them, unless they are labeled; while on the other hand to come upon a constant repetition of "said he," "said she," "said Tom," "said Jane," is as irritating as bumping over a corduroy bridge in a cart without springs. It is worth the author's while to take all possible pains to give explicit indication of the personality of the speaker wherever this is needed and equally to omit it where it is superfluous. Here is an example from a second-rate novel:—

"I'm off on Monday," said he.

"Not really," said she.

"Yes, I have only come to say good-by," said he.

"Shall you be gone long?" asked she.

"That depends," said he.

"I should like to know what takes you away," said she.

"I dare say," said he, smiling.

"I shouldn't wonder if I know," said she.

"I dare say you might guess," said he.

There are so many devices for avoiding repetition that only gross carelessness can commit a fault like this. The abundance of terms which may be used—said, remarked, observed, replied, returned, retorted, asked, inquired, demanded, murmured, grumbled, growled, sneered, explained, exclaimed, and the rest of the long list of words of allied meanings—leaves the writer of English without excuse if he fail to vary the words of specification in dialogue. There are, too, many ways of evading the need of employing any of these. Frequently the nature of the talk indicates sufficiently the speaker; and it is often possible and well to introduce the name of the character addressed. The simple device of altering the relative position of the verb and the subject is not to be despised. In the extract just given the ear would receive as a relief and a boon a single "he said" among so many "said he's." Opening Stevenson's "Treasure Island" almost at random, and taking the words on a couple of pages which indicate the speakers and their utterances, I find these:—

Observed Silver.... Cried the cook.... Returned Morgan.... Said another.... Cried Silver.... Said Merry.... Agreed Silver.... Said Morgan.... Said the fellow with the bandage.... Observed another.

On a couple of pages of one of Hardy's books the phrases are:—

Said a young married man.... Murmured Joseph.... Dashed in Mark Clark.... Added Joseph.... Said Henry.... Observed Mr. Mark.... Whispered Joseph.... Said Mr. Oak.... Continued Joseph.

The variety does not come by chance, but by care and a finely trained perception of the value of trifles. It is of importance that the exact significance and intensity of the verb employed be taken into account. There is a distinct difference between "dashed in" and "continued;" between "cried" and "exclaimed." The author should have a sense of the mood and manner of his personages so clear and so fine that only one of all the possible words shall seem to him fit. If his dialogue is at all related to real life, it will so vary in its fine shadings that the terms indicating the manner of utterance will vary naturally and inevitably.

The interspersion of comments in dialogues is another matter of detail which greatly increases or lessens the finish of work. It is often possible to give a much more lively and vivid presentation of the speakers if amid their talk are mixed bits of action or even of description. The two things to be observed are that there shall not be too much of this and that the interpolations shall be significant. The movement of the current of conversation must not be hindered. Trifles may be effectively used, yet it is one of the most difficult points of literary art so to use them. It is a good thing for the student to write little sketches in dialogue form; stories in which he is forced to depend almost entirely upon the talk itself for characterization and narrative. Readers as a rule do not care much for this sort of thing, and it is to be done as part of the training of the workman rather than for itself. To sum up this matter, it may be said that in interspersing comment, as in all else that has to do with dialogue, the great secret lies in realizing the persons speaking and in allowing them to utter their own words, instead of making them speak the words of the author or stand aside while the author expresses his thoughts himself.

XIX

Character and Purpose

The secret of character-drawing of course lies largely in the ability to understand and to appreciate character, but in its application to practical work it largely resolves itself into the power of realizing the personages of the tale. A striking example of how a vitalizing imagination can and may make the actors in a fiction real in spite of all drawbacks is furnished by George Meredith. George Meredith's style is a teasing madness; his characters talk as no human beings ever dreamed of talking; and yet these personages are so actual, so individual, so human, that it is impossible not to feel that if one of them were pricked, real, red, warm human blood would flow. They existed so vividly for the author that they exist vividly for the reader and convince in spite of all the author's mannerisms. The relation of an author to his puppets has been well put by Trollope when he says:—

> The novelist has other aims than the elucidation of his plot. He desires to make his readers so intimately acquainted with his characters that the creatures of his brain should be to them speaking, moving, living, human creatures. This he can never do unless he know those fictitious personages himself, and he can never know them unless he can live with them in the full reality of established intimacy.... He must learn to hate them and to love them. He must argue with them, quarrel with them, forgive them, and even submit to them.—*Autobiography*, xiii.

Deliberate description of persons is seldom of much effect. Says Stevenson:—

> Readers cannot fail to have remarked that what an author tells us of the beauty or the charm of his creatures goes for naught; that we know instantly better; that the heroine cannot open her mouth but what, all

in a moment, the fine phrases of preparation fall from her like the robes from Cinderella, and she stands before us, self-betrayed, as a poor, ugly, sickly wench, or perhaps a strapping market-woman.—*A Gossip on a Novel of Dumas's.*

The same principle holds with mental traits. It is of little use to announce, and especially to announce early in a tale, what the character of an actor is. If the author declare that the fictitious person is this or that, he gives the reader a measure by which to criticise his performance. He puts into the hands of his public a rod wherewith to scourge him for whatever falls short of intention,—and if tried for falling short of intention, who shall escape? If the reader is left to judge of character by deeds, he becomes himself responsible for any opinions which he may choose to hold. The rule which every student should adopt for himself is that character is to be indicated first by the acts of the personages in a tale, and secondly by their talk. Description of character may be suggested, but it should not be direct if it is possible to avoid this.

Of course I do not mean that there may not be a good deal of direct comment on character. I do mean, however, that while it will probably entertain the author to write this and may help him in understanding the people about whom he writes, the effect upon the reader will in most cases be exceedingly small. If you are in the habit of analyzing your mental experiences, I am confident that you will bear me out in saying that we are seldom much affected by any declaration on the part of the writer that a character is good, bad, or indifferent. If we have drawn the same conclusion from the story, that is from the events and the conversations, we may agree with the author; if we have not, we do not in the least accept his estimate.

This may seem a covert attack upon the whole school of analytical fiction, but it is meant merely to be a warning to practical workers. There is nothing in all literary art more enticing to a novelist than the vivisection of character, and especially in this introspective age is it difficult to write objectively and without what might be called mental rummaging. It is impossible not to feel that all this minute analysis of character, however interesting as psychological tract or treatise, distinctly injures the effect of a work as a whole. It changes the characters from living beings to subjects on the dissecting-table, and destroys the vitality of the tale. It is in our time the prevailing fashion, but it is of our time no less the literary disease. In the masterpieces of fiction it is seldom found; and the book which is heavily weighted with analysis is desperately sure of going soon to the bottom of the pool of oblivion, no matter by how much wit or wisdom it may be buoyed up.

Often a single significant detail will throw more light on a character than pages of comment. An example in perfection is the phrase in which Thackeray tells how Becky Crawley, amid all her guilt and terror, when her husband had Lord Steyne by the throat, felt a sudden thrill of admiration for Rawdon's splendid strength. It is like a flash of lightning which shows the deeps of the selfish, sensual woman's nature. It is no wonder that Thackeray threw down his pen, as he confessed that he did, and cried, "That is a stroke of genius!"

Of drawing characters from life much the same may be said as in regard to taking incidents from life. Real characters are excellent points of departure, and in the study of mental traits it is possible to hold much more closely to nature than in the reproduction of incidents. It is easy to pass the line of probability in incident, but one may go far before he cross the line of probability in character. It follows that there is in character much more material which may be taken directly from life into fiction, without especial modification. The chief difficulty here is—or at least so it seems to me—that it is less easy to make an actual person real in the mind as part of a fiction than it is to realize a person practically imaginary. If the writer in his thought and imagination get as perfect a conviction of a personage in his story when he is drawing him directly from life as when he shapes him from pure imagination, there is no reason why he should not use the living man as his model, and often he may in this way gain greater consistency of development.

Character-drawing belongs rather to novels than to short stories. The short story practically deals with character as it shows itself in a crisis or in a brief and rapid series of events. There is here no great opportunity for showing the development of character, but only for exhibiting how character is manifested under crucial and significant circumstances. The method must be varied according to the conditions, and almost perforce the writer of the short tale is forced to deal chiefly in suggestion, both of outward and inner conditions and traits, rather than in extended exposition. In any case, however, the same fundamental principle holds, that the clearness of the impression produced upon the reader depends upon the command of technical methods which enables a writer to impart what he feels and upon the sharpness with which he realizes the character he depicts.

When there is talk of moral purpose in fiction most persons are either a little indignant or a good deal inclined to get out of the way. If they think how much useless talk has been wasted over the phrase they are impatient; if they recall how dull much of this talk has been, they are bored by the very idea. Indeed, one is sometimes tempted to take refuge in mere flippancy, and to try to shut off discussion by declaring that while it is true that there was formerly such a thing as moral purpose in literature this has in these degenerate days entirely given place to an immoral purpose. Yet despite this impatience the fact remains that the matter is one of the most important connected with the art of fiction.

What is generally meant by the question whether a story shall have a moral purpose is whether it shall convey an avowed lesson, whether, in short, it shall be undisguisedly or at least deliberately didactic. To this there seems to me but one answer possible, whether from a literary or an ethical point of view,—and that is an unqualified negative. From the point of view of political and social economics it might appear that this statement is too sweeping, but closer examination, I believe, shows it to be sound. Take, for instance, "Uncle Tom's Cabin," a book which has been at least as widely read as any ever produced in this country. Whatever may have been the opinion in the quarter of the century in which the book saw the light, it would probably be impossible to find to-day a critic of reputation who would place it above mediocrity considered simply as literature.

As a means of aiding a great social reform it is one of the most noteworthy intellectual productions of the time. Its reputation was of course due largely to the accidental association with a great political movement, but its influence makes it a historical document of the highest possible interest. From the literary point of view its moral purpose is a mistake, and is a drag upon it; just as the question of the reform of the Court of Chancery is a drag upon "Bleak House." We may admire the reformatory effects of these novels, but our interest in this is historical in so far as it exists at all.

When the critics took Mrs. Humphry Ward to task for so heavily freighting "Robert Elsmere" with metaphysical discussion and disquisition, that lady published a defense of her methods. She declared that she could not "try to reflect the time without taking account of forces which are at least as real and living as other forces, and have as much to do with the drama of human existence." She misses the real point. She assumes that the objection is to the choice of subject which she has made in writing her book. The trouble is not simply that she has concerned herself with theological scruples. It is that she has made her moral obvious as a moral; and, what is of perhaps even more importance, that she has not the art to make her theme show through it the fundamentally human emotions with which, and with which only, art is properly concerned. It is not the province of art to deal with the question of limited interests except as they depend upon and illustrate human life in its wide meaning. Art cannot stop at so confined an inquiry as whether a man shall be a Mohammedan, a Catholic, or a Protestant or an Agnostic. The novelist who would succeed permanently must go deeper than that. The essential principle of conviction which is common to all humanity must be shown through the conflict between differing creeds. Here the matter is that of emotions and principles general to all men, although the especial circumstances in which these are exercised may be particular and individual. In so far as "Robert Elsmere" is significant of that passionate fidelity to truth which is respected by all mankind it is vital and significant; but it is mistaken and transient in so far as it is concerned with the discussion of accidental rather than with general truth. I use "accidental" here in a purely literary sense. I am not estimating the value of creeds. I mean simply to say that all men as human beings are not interested in the question whether Agnosticism or the Church of England is to be preferred; while every true man is concerned with the fact that it often costs much for a human being to follow his most profound inner conviction.

This brings me to what I should say is the first principle involved in this matter. Literature as an art should deal with those ethical questions only which are of universal human interest.

We have noticed already that whatever a reader is led to do for himself is more real and more vital than anything which can be done for him. This principle, carried farther and higher, underlies the fact that mankind will give little heed to any "record of intellectual conceptions" of life, while they will be moved and led by a "reflection of life"—in other words by those tales which are the embodiment of human emotions and human passions. To be told what some man thinks that life should mean to us may interest but is not likely to move us deeply or to change us. To be shown, vitally and vividly, what life has meant to any human being can hardly fail to reach our emotions and to affect the whole mental being. Life can teach more than any man can teach. The novelist who preaches is tacitly assuming that his individual belief is of more value than the inferences which a reader would draw from a faithful picture of life. The race avenges itself upon such an egotist. It does not reason about it, but it lets his book die. Where is the didactic novel that has outlived its generation? To be didactic is at best to be temporary.

The very essence of all art is that the motive of a work shall be inherent in it and not an outside purpose; but even aside from this, the moral purpose which shows itself as such defeats its own object. The lesson which is elaborated for us belongs in the sermon, and sermons are apt to be of effect so transient that it is necessary to have a fresh one at least once a week. The teaching of a genuine work of art is permanent. It is hardly conceivable that the race should outlive the teaching of Dante or Shakespeare. The hypothesis upon which the "moral purpose," so called, is introduced into fiction is that men shall be moved to accept its teaching. The objection which it seems fair to urge against this is that the ethical lesson conveyed indirectly is so much more effectual; and that it is not wise to waste the opportunity and to dull men's minds to the legitimate effects of fiction.

What the sincere novelist does is practically to say to his reader: "Here is a portion of life as it seems to me it is or might be. I tell you the whole of its reality or its possibility as far as I can perceive it. What it means, what is the lesson to be drawn from it, you must discover for yourself. In the first place the emotions which I have felt in writing the tale cannot be directly expressed. I have endeavored to suggest them, and that is all that can be done by means of language. In the second place, the moral of life will be vital only to him who draws it for himself." Of course it is impossible to determine how far one novelist or another would definitely say to himself anything of this sort; but I believe that this is the position consciously or unconsciously taken by every serious writer of fiction.

No conviction, no opinion, no faith is vital which is not the original growth of the mind which holds it. We may induce it. We may advance ideas, we may even formulate views, and suppose that we have converted another to our own position, be it intellectual, moral, æsthetic, or religious. We may have secured a sort of conformity; the other may even himself suppose that he thinks as we do; but until he feels that we think as he does there is little hope that genuine opinions have taken root in his mind. It is only when the life within him has consciously put into tangible form its own belief that he is in any permanent way, in any real sense, convinced. Conviction which is forced upon one by deliberately didactic books is like a costume, assumed willingly or unwillingly as the case may be, but only an outer covering. Conviction which is wrought in one by inner emotion in reading the story of Arthur Pendennis, of Colonel Newcome, of Effie Deans, of Jean Valjean, of Hester Prynne, is a change in the very fibre of the moral being. The one is a view, and the other is vitality; one is a theory, and the other is belief; the one is a creed, but the other is character.

XX

Translation

As the intimate intercourse of the inhabitants of the earth increases, the necessity of setting over literature from one tongue to another is every day greater. One nation is no longer content with its own science or its own literature. Each is greedy for the intellectual treasures of the whole race. Whatever of thought, of experience, of imagination has been recorded by the men of any country, is of interest to the readers of all, and there is therefore a steadily increasing demand for versions of foreign books.

Translation has come to be almost a distinct profession. The increased exercise of the art has raised greatly the standard of excellence demanded. It is true that there is still a great deal of slipshod work offered to the public, but even cheapness is ceasing to be an effectual recommendation for bad translations when good ones are to be had. It is now necessary for the writer who makes this his business to learn his trade pretty thoroughly. The days of schoolboy renderings are about over, and some translators, like Miss Katherine Wormeley, have raised their work to so high a level that it is almost entitled to take rank with original production.

Translation is in the mind of the general public associated with rendering into extremely scraggly English the "Commentaries" of Cæsar or the "Æneid" of Virgil. Most of us have been through experiences like that of Betty in "A Woodland Wooing:"—

"Just listen to this stuff. I've got the rest of it, but I can't make head or tail out of this."

"Well, what is it?" demanded Bob.

"'Him likewise perchance furious alike impelling, and the spoils of the Ægean deity whatsoever by means of madness notwithstanding to be about to be sacrificed.' There, that is the very best I can make out of it."

"Well," returned Bob, with brotherly candor, "you *are* a muff. That's plain enough. Don't you see: 'He also declared himself about to be sacrificed, an offering to the insatiate Ægean deity; not caring to live, moreover, impelled by furious madness, but ready alike to finish and be forgotten.' That is as easy as rolling off a log."—Ch. iii.

This idea, however, it is needful to lay aside if the subject is to be discussed intelligibly, for Translation has come to be treated as a serious matter, and to be developed like any other intellectual pursuit.

The first fact to be accepted in considering Translation is that it is impossible exactly to render into one language what has been written in another. The race that has made each tongue has impressed its own character upon it in every syllable, in every idiom. It is not difficult to repeat in one speech the general idea of what is said in another, and for practical purposes this is often all that is required. The directions for making a machine, the particulars of a shipment of grain, the questions one asks in shopping may with no especial difficulty be changed from language to language. When it comes to thoughts, and still more when emotions are to be dealt with, it is impossible to give in two tongues precisely the same shade of meaning. The delicate aroma of a piece of literary art is as surely diminished or lost in translation as a man becomes a foreigner and noticeably strange when removed from his own country to another. Even in practical affairs this is sometimes a serious consideration. The meaning in different languages of the phrases most nearly equivalent is so far from being identical that in important treaties between nations of differing speech it is necessary to agree beforehand what tongue shall be considered authoritative in case of dispute. In scientific books it is common to find that a translator is forced to add the original to his version of some sentence or phrase because there is no exact equivalent. Words cannot completely express thought in any case, and to this constant infirmity of language is in translation added the difficulty that the words of one tongue cannot accurately represent the precise shade of idea phrased by another.

Professor Wendell remarks:—

Each language names ideas in a way peculiarly its own. The common agreement on arbitrary symbols that at length results in the vocabulary of any language is sure to produce symbols that stand for peculiar aspects of real thoughts and emotions which language tries to define,—for aspects in other words which differ from those named by any other tongue; and what is thus plainly true of words by themselves is just as true of words in combination.... In its vocabulary, in its grammar, in its entirety, each language must express the lasting meaning of life in aspects different from those expressed by any other.—*Stelligeri*, p. 103.

It follows that the best that a translator can hope to do is to give the nearest approximation to the original that the language into which he is changing it is capable of. The problem is not unlike that of the engraver who is endeavoring to reproduce a picture painted with the brush. At every point he is forced to decide what combination of lines and spaces will best represent the work before him. He knows that it is impossible by any arrangement of lines actually to reproduce the brush-work of the painter, and so he goes on considering what effect among those within his reach most nearly approaches this.

The methods of the translator of course vary with the nature of the original with which he has to deal. In rendering documents which have to do with practical affairs the chief consideration is strict exactness of idea. If one attempts to translate a scientific treatise, the most important point is absolute accuracy. It is in any case necessary to write correct and clear English, but Force and Elegance may for the moment be left practically out of consideration,—or, rather, are considered as in importance subordinate to Clearness. To say in our tongue as precisely as possible what the author has said in his is the translator's first care, and to express, too, the material, literal, scientific meaning of this as it would appear to a reader of the original. Here there is no question of atmosphere, of suggestion, of connotation. The emotional element of literature may and indeed must be ignored here. The intellectual quality is the only thing to be regarded.

All this is comparatively easy. If one knows the languages from which and into which he is translating, he should have no especial difficulty in changing a scientific paper from one to another. His knowledge of the subject will of course affect the ease and accuracy of the result; and of course the comparative richness of the scientific vocabulary of the languages is to be taken into account. In general terms, however, this sort of translation calls for the exercise of the intellectual faculties only; and whatever depends upon the intellect may be acquired by any one who has an intellect, if he choose to take the trouble.

When it is a question of a version in another tongue of literature in its higher sense the matter at once becomes more complicated. Here there is not only the idea to be considered, but the suggestion, the flavor, the peculiar quality of style and individuality. There must be an attempt to give some impression of the effect produced in the original by euphony, by what we speak of as word-color, meaning thereby the melody and the peculiar quality which terms have from suggestions so subtle that it is all but impossible to analyze them. All these requirements thrust themselves upon the translator, and he must struggle to achieve the impossible in transferring these from one language to the other. The difficulties of the undertaking are well illustrated by George Henry Lewes, in the following passage:—

> Words are not only symbols of objects, but centres of associations; and their suggestiveness depends partly upon their sound. Thus there is not the slightest difference in meaning expressed when I say, "The dews of night began to fall," or, "The nightly dews commenced to fall." Meaning and metre are the same; but one is poetry, the other prose. Wordsworth paints a landscape in this line:—
>
> The river wanders at its own sweet will.
>
> Let us translate it into other words: "The river runneth free from all restraint." We preserve the meaning, but where is the landscape? Or

we may turn it thus, "The river flows, now here, now there, at will," which is a very close translation, much closer than any usually found in a foreign language, where, indeed, it would in all probability assume some such form as this, "The river, self-impelled, pursues its course." In these examples we have what is seldom found in translations, accuracy of meaning expressed in similar metre; yet the music and the poetry are gone, because the music and the poetry are organically dependent upon certain peculiar arrangements of sound and suggestion.—*Life of Goethe*, 2d ed., p. 466. Quoted in Genung's "Practical Rhetoric."

It is in the rendering of works which belong to that department of literature to which is given the name belles-lettres that translation is most difficult and also most common. Poetry, fiction, essays, and kindred forms are most frequently the subject of the worker at this craft. Here the form is often of importance as great as that of the idea. To give merely a literal version of the exact ideas in the original would do no more toward reproducing it than a photograph does toward reproducing the Sistine Madonna or a plaster cast the Venus of Melos. Indeed, of the formally literal translation it is hardly too much to say that it really represents the original no more than a collection of paint-tubes containing all the colors in a painting would represent the picture. The value in the painting lies in the manner in which the tints have been arranged and varied, blended here and contrasted there. In literature, the value lies in the cunning blending and contrasting, the arrangement and variety with which ideas are presented. Shelley said of the chant of the archangels which opens the "Prologue in Heaven" of Goethe's "Faust" that not only is it "impossible to represent in another language the melody of the versification," but that "even the volatile strength and delicacy of the ideas escape in the crucible of translation." Every one who has attempted to translate a work of imaginative merit must appreciate this.

Of course, the first thing which a translator considers is the setting over of the ideas from one tongue to another, yet it seems to me a great mistake to make first a version which is simply literal, and then to try to mould it over into forms of literary grace. Of course, this is a matter which must to a certain extent depend upon individual temperament, but it is certainly true here as in other work that a phrase or a sentence can be more readily shaped and modified while it is fresh than when it has cooled and hardened. Translation is no mechanical operation, and no mechanical excellence will suffice. It is therefore well to aim at excellence of quality from the first, instead of attempting to add it as it were by an afterthought.

The first and essential requisite in making a translation is that it be English. By this is meant not only that it shall be made up of English words. It is not even sufficient that it be made up of English words so arranged that they may be understood. It is necessary that the English shall be sound and idiomatic. The ideal translation preserves nothing in its style to indicate that it was not originally written in the tongue in which it stands. It is the aim of the translator to approximate as closely to this standard of excellence as he is able. The sentence-structure of the German is more elaborate and more extended than our own. It is necessary that the translator of German works do not model his English version after this peculiarity of the original. The paragraph structure of the French is peculiarly broken and brief; yet the writer who sets work over from French into English is not permitted to let this fact determine the manner of his paragraphing in the latter language. Still more important is it that the idiom of the alien speech shall not leave its traces upon the style of the translation. This is the point in which all mechanical training fails. A friend gave me the other day a copy of the sign which was placed above the electric-light button in the chamber that he occupied in a hotel at Geneva: "One is begged on entering the room to press the button to let the light, and on parting again to extend it." The man who wrote this rather remarkable direction knew his vocabulary tolerably well, but he had no idea of the English idiom. You have all of you seen innumerable examples of the same sort of blunder, and it is one which can be avoided only by an intimate acquaintance with the tongue into which one is translating.

Of the three great languages with which the translator is likely to have to do, French is by far the most idiomatic, German the least, while English in this respect stands midway between the other two. The problem in dealing with idioms is to find in one tongue expressions which are rather the equivalents of the original than a literal translation. The most nearly satisfactory renderings of the plays of Aristophanes which are to be found in our literature are those of John Hookham Frere, and they are probably among the least literal. Aristophanes was one of the most idiomatic of classic authors, and he indulged in slang as well as in idiom. To give an impression at all approximating to that of the original it is necessary constantly to depart from the exact words of the Greek text, especially when an attempt is made to preserve the feeling of the metrical effects of the comedies. In "The Birds," the literal meaning of a certain passage is this: "Come ... as many as in the furrows incessantly twitter around the clods so lightly with blithesome voice." This is rendered by Frere:—

Rioting on the furrowed plain,

Pecking, hopping,

Picking, popping,

Among the barley newly sown.

The difference between the literal version and the other is that from the latter the reader gets something of the impression which the Greek carried to its auditors, while from the former nothing is to be obtained beyond the plain and exact meaning.

Those who have examined the translation of the "Phormio" which was furnished to the audience when that play was acted at Harvard in 1894 found there numerous illustrations of this use of equivalents in place of exact meaning. The character of the dialogue made it proper to employ modern slang to give the impression which the original conveyed to the audience for which it was written. Accordingly the Latin phrase which literally means "Gird up your loins" was translated "Brace up!" "Bring the old man" was rendered "Trot out your old man!"

"Now what will be the talk of folk?" is made to read "Why, what will Mrs. Grundy say?" The whole is an amusing though perhaps somewhat extreme example of the modern idea of translating by the emotional equivalent instead of by the literal equivalent; of giving the phrase which shall make on the English-speaking reader the impression made by the original upon the reader who spoke the tongue in which the work was first written.

The method of turning foreign works into English which has until recently been the popular one is admirably illustrated by the versions of German novels which have been so successfully made by Mrs. A. L. Wister. Mrs. Wister once said to a young woman who applied to her for aid in getting translating to do, and who justified her application upon the ground that she was an excellent French and German scholar: "That is not the question. The thing is whether you are able to write English well. Anybody can find out the meaning of a French or German text; that is simply a matter of using a grammar and a dictionary. The secret of making an acceptable translation lies in the ability to express that meaning in good English." This is admirably said, but it does not cover the whole ground. It is of the first importance that the translator write good English, but it is hardly to be supposed that the use of grammar and lexicon will give a writer that intimate and sympathetic acquaintance with foreign idioms without which it is impossible to make a version satisfactory in the modern sense.

Mrs. Wister is an excellent example of what might more correctly be called a "paraphraser" than a "translator." It has been her custom to select some popular German novel, and from that to make a story which seemed to her likely to please the American public. She has allowed herself the widest liberty, even to the extent, if I am not misinformed, of suppressing characters and modifying situations which did not please her, or of otherwise altering the story in important particulars. The success with which her books have met has justified her practical wisdom in adopting this method of following literature as a bread-winning business. She set out to please the average story-reader, by providing for the market pleasantly exciting, clean, and entertaining books. She has done it well, and she has achieved the end she sought.

There is always in the mind of the literary man some doubt how far one author has the moral right thus to bejuggle the work of another, even in translation. One who has written cannot help being influenced by a sort of sub-consciousness of what his own feelings would be if a translator were to work such a transformation upon one of his books. Letting this pass, however, it is to be said that popular demands in regard to the quality and veracity of translations have steadily advanced. The paraphraser is now forced to appeal to a public intellectually lower than that he formerly addressed. The literary grade of the admirers of Mrs. Wister's books is probably distinctly below what it was ten years ago. Her school may be said practically to have had its day; and the translator in the best sense has taken the place of the paraphraser.

It is not that the translator may not take liberties, as we have already seen in speaking of idiom. It is that where before liberties were taken for the pleasure or from the caprice of the paraphraser, variations are now supposed to be made by the translator for the sole purpose of imparting to the reader a better idea of the impression produced by the original on those who read it in its first form. Miss Wormeley, for instance, is publishing a version of the comedies of Molière. She has decided that she can give the American reader who is unacquainted with French a better idea of the plays by rendering them into prose than by attempting the rhymed verse of the original. To the average American of to-day the effect is undoubtedly more satisfactory than that of any metrical version could be. This is an extreme instance, and it involves the difficulty of retaining the beauties and value of poetical forms in translation, but it illustrates the length to which variations from the original may legitimately go if they are made in the line of fidelity to the impression of the original.

The two great principles in translation, then, are faithfulness to the impression produced by the work in its own language, and faithfulness to the tongue into which it is rendered, especially in idiomatic constructions. It is to be remembered that the difficulty of producing a satisfactory version is never an excuse for any failure. The fact that one undertakes to make a translation is equivalent to a profession of ability to cope with whatever obstacles the task may present.

The value of translating as a help toward literary facility is a thing which should not be overlooked by the student. Whatever increases ease in the handling of language is of worth, and especially valuable is whatever forces the writer to greater exactness in the use of words and phrases. Reading aloud in English from a book in another language is excellent practice in the line of training the mind to quickness in the use of words; and this is especially good for one going into newspaper work.

It is going a little out of our way to comment here on the translation which comes into school work, but a word may not be amiss. It is always to be remembered, both by teacher and by pupil, that translation involves two languages, and one as fully as the other. Too often work of this sort is done as if the foreign language was the one to be considered exclusively. Students are allowed to give an approximate meaning of the Latin or the French which they are reading, putting their so-called translation into a verbal jargon which uses the English vocabulary, but which is no more English than the dictionary becomes a poem from having in it the words used in poetry. This is unfair to the student in several ways. It makes him hate what he is doing; it prevents his ever having anything like a proper or true idea of the value of the literature which he is mangling out of a foreign tongue into mongrel English. It destroys his feeling for his own language, and it makes it all but impossible for him to be taught English composition. More than one teacher who agonizes in spirit over the themes of his or her pupils, wondering why it is seemingly so impossible to teach them to write even reasonably well, might find an answer to the perplexing question by considering the English into which they are allowed to render their work in the languages. If pupils are let to translate from French and German and Latin into a sort of schoolroom dialect, inexact, unidiomatic, and lifeless, it is gross stupidity to expect that they will fail to be influenced by this. A pupil's education is a unit. As long as it is assumed that his training in the languages is one thing, in mathematics another, and in geography or history a third, there is a constant loss of energy in counteracting the effects of this mistake. Every branch must be taught with a view to every other, and learned with a view to every other; and especially evident is it that in all teaching the matter of the proper use of the language of the learner should be kept always in sight. The translation which injures the pupil's use of his own tongue does him a harm which cannot be atoned for by any knowledge it gives him of another.

It must by this time be apparent that translation in the best sense is really so closely allied to original work as hardly to be distinguished from it. In fact no writer can hope to produce successful versions of works of imagination who has not himself a genuine literary gift, carefully trained. The pathetic idea of so many young women that because they have taken lessons in French and German they can make their living by translating from those languages is quickly and painfully crushed by any attempt to carry it into practice; but there is far from being any adequate conception even among general writers of how difficult an art really good translation is. Yet so rapidly is public taste being educated in this matter that poor versions from other tongues become every day more and more futile and ineffective.

XXI

Criticism

Criticism is the estimation of work by defined standards. In its application to literature it is the trying of whatever is written. It is, so to say, the balance-sheet of composition.

Criticism is a sort of Exposition, yet it is well to consider it by itself because it has so much the nature of a general survey of the whole field of composition. Indeed, since literary training depends so largely upon self-criticism, it is essential to understand its methods and principles before one can hope to progress fast or far.

There has never before been a time when there has been so much talk about the art as in the latter half of this century, and seldom a time when there has been less of the genuine article. Matthew Arnold preached the gospel of criticism, and the world went on its uncritical way very much as before. There have even been doubts expressed whether there was after all any such thing save in theory. That entertaining Philistine, Mr. Andrew Lang, has declared that criticism is nothing but the expression of personal opinion, and has strengthened his position by pretty consistently living up to the assertion. The definition has been somewhat widely accepted; and it is certainly true that much which in common speech is called criticism is nothing more or less than an expression of prejudice or opinion. Indeed, in common speech the word is pretty generally used to signify mere fault-finding. There is, however, no more propriety in using the verb "to criticise" in the sense of "to censure" than in the sense of "to praise." It means neither. Its nearest synonym is "to estimate," or "to measure."

Criticism is appreciation based upon comparison of work with defined standards. To criticise is to form or to express an opinion.

It is as far from blame on the one hand as from praise on the other; but it establishes the reason for either. As a branch of Exposition it is a written estimate. The principles of the art are the same whatever is the nature of the work to which judgment is applied, but we shall speak of it here chiefly as applied to literature.

The first necessity in criticism is that of a standard. Without definite standards there can be no measurement of work. There is no estimating the truth or falsity of anything unless there is first some idea of truth; the merit or the worthlessness of a thing cannot be measured unless there be some ideal by which it may be judged. Until one has personal standards by which to measure life he cannot be said to have any moral identity; until he has standards by which to estimate ideas, he has no intellectual identity; until he has definite and defined standards by which to criticise literature it is hardly possible to consider that he has literary identity or that he is entitled to lay claim to any literary opinion as his own.

I have spoken in a former lecture of that irritating class who take refuge behind the phrase, "I do not know what is good or bad, but I know what I like." The phrase is a confession of either mental incapacity or of mental slothfulness. It means either "I am too stupid to think out the reason why this pleases me," or "I am too lazy to think." It is a moral duty for one to know why one likes or dislikes a thing. I do not mean that we can go to the ultimate analysis of the reasons why beauty delights and ugliness pains. I do mean that the possession of reason lays on a man a moral obligation to use it; and that so far as his individual reason can go, it is his duty to examine the grounds of his feelings. How is a man to have the courage of his dislikes if he does not know upon what they rest? It is the duty of every rational creature to have opinions. In order to have opinions it is necessary to estimate belief and feeling. In order to estimate it is needful to have standards.

All this being so, how are standards to be obtained? There is unfortunately no market where they are to be bought; and the mere mention of acquiring them fills untrained and timorous minds with a shuddering sense of horribly laborious undertaking. Yet in its plainest form the matter is simply to know what one believes; and that is the first step in any mental development which can claim to be genuine. This does not mean that criticism is to be a matter of personal opinion in the sense of its being arbitrary liking or disliking. It means that the first standard by which all work must be tried is that of its truth; and that to be able to measure its truth it is necessary to know what one regards as truth. To be able to estimate the verity of a book it is essential that one have definite opinions in regard to the truth as it concerns life and humanity, and that one be not in the least in doubt what those opinions are. Criticism by vague opinions is like weight by an uncertain balance.

For individual criticism, moreover, it is absolutely essential that judgment be made by truth as it appears to the critic, and not by his idea of what others may think to be truth. His knowledge of what others believe is to influence him in establishing a standard, not in his measurement of works by it. In other words, we all are and should be affected in our decision of what is truth by the opinion of our fellow-men. When we have made up our mind that a certain thing is true, we try work by it as a standard without reference to the belief or the disbelief of others.

This is a matter which reaches far. It seems to me that it is hardly possible to insist too strongly in education upon the need of realizing one's opinions. What many persons call their mind is merely a sort of mental protoplasm from which a mind may with care be developed, and the most effective means of development is that of defining clearly the things which we believe and of assuring ourselves as exactly as may be what to us is and what is not truth.

Our idea of truth is the standard by which we estimate the thing that a work expresses, whether in idea or in impression. To estimate the mechanics of a book, its technical finish, and all that has to do with workmanship, it is necessary to study the masterpieces of literature. To judge of what may be done and what may therefore be fairly demanded, it is necessary to examine those works which have stood the test of time and which are pronounced good by the verdict of mankind. It is difficult to form our standards from contemporary writings because in them what is permanent is apt to be obscured by the temporary. Literature shows the relation of men to their time and the relation of man to life. In the classics of all languages, in the books which have lived from generation to generation, the temporary drops out of sight while the essential remains. A story which showed the relation of the men of the Restoration to the great struggle between Puritanism and Royalty was of poignant and even bitter interest to the readers of that time because each reader was a partisan on one side or on the other. To-day we have no personal feeling in regard to these political and religious differences, which without the aid of foot-notes we very likely do not even understand. Only the essential and human remains. We read such a tale with a perception only of the revelation which it makes of the nature of permanent human emotions. We get from it only the truths which have to do with the relation of man to life, not as it is for one party or sect, but as it is for man as a human being. When "Uncle Tom's Cabin" was new, it was hardly possible to look at it from a literary standpoint, because from one side or the other of the great anti-slavery question its readers felt passionately its moral purpose. We are already far enough away from the anti-slavery struggle to be able to examine the book critically, and to decide upon its literary qualities without reference to its political or moral weight. It is only when time has practically eliminated the temporary and accidental in a work that we are able to look at it in a temper dispassionate enough to allow us to get from it an idea of the essential qualities which shall be to us a standard.

The things which we are thus to learn from the study of the masterpieces and the classics of literature, are: first, the laws of province, and second, the possibilities of literary expression. By the laws of province—which is a somewhat formidable name for a not very complicated thing—I mean what is the province of each variety of literary form. This would include, for instance, the consideration of the consistency of fairy tales, the discussion of a moral purpose in fiction, methods in writing history or biography, and all the many matters of this nature. If we are to consider how well a novelist has done his work, it is necessary that we have some clearly defined notion of what comes properly within the scope of a novel; if we are to criticise a romance, a history, an essay, it is in any case needful that we be acquainted with what the experience of permanent literature and the judgment of the masters have decided to be the proper range of each sort of writing. This is what is meant by the laws of province. It is only by the careful study of the best works of these several sorts that we become qualified to judge how far a new production holds by the laws which should govern a composition of its kind. This is the more difficult as these laws are largely unwritten, and from the nature of things must be differently applied in different cases.

One thing must be said in regard to the authority of the classics, the masterpieces of literature to which we are to go to learn our standards. The young author is apt to feel that it is a mark of weakness to confess that he is influenced by the example of those who have gone before him. He protests, often pretty vigorously, against this autocratic rule of authors long since dust strewn as far as waters flow or the wind speeds. He feels that it is for the living to make laws for the living, and this generally means in his own case a willingness to make such canons, or at least a determination to be a law unto himself. The difficulty is that he does not recognize the true state of things. The domain of literature is not a despotism, but the most absolutely free of all republics. No author, no matter how great he be, can force the public to accept his book or can impose his works upon the generations. It is by the suffrages of the readers of the world that he stands or falls, and if there was ever given in the whole world a disinterested and impartial vote, it is precisely this decision which the world makes upon the merit of works. What we call the classics are the books which the world has decided are good. It is the consensus of the opinion of mankind that dominates here. The opinion of individuals is often wrong. I doubt if the verdict of generations upon a book ever errs substantially.

Yet another thought is of importance. To write is to endeavor to communicate thought. It is manifestly inconsistent and illogical not to choose that method of communication to which the world will listen. The measure of the world's willingness is to be found in the works which the world has permanently approved. We learn our standards from the masterpieces of literature, we say; we might say: Here are the books which show what form of composition will be attended to by the world which the writer wishes to address. To see how far successful a given author has been in doing what he attempted, it is well to compare his work with this.

The forming of standards of mechanical excellence is of course founded on the same principles as those by which we determine what I have called the laws of province. There is no hard-and-fast rule by which to define exactly the limits of one department of literature or another, and the only thing which can without qualification be said is that no one can write criticisms which are of any lasting or indeed of any transient value who is not well acquainted with the great body of good English literature.

One thing should be kept constantly in mind in writing criticisms, and that is that the critic must appreciate and hold to the point of view of the author criticised. The great point is to know what the author tried to do, and to judge how far he has succeeded in doing it. If a book is written for the general public, for instance, it is manifestly unfair to complain that it does not meet the needs of the specialists; and equally would it be unfair to find fault with the volume carefully prepared for the specialist for not being adapted to the average reader. Be sure that in writing a criticism you are clear in regard to what it is proper to expect from a given book, and in regard also to what the work is or is not as judged by the standard thus established. Criticism must first of all things be definite.

One of the powers first to be called into play in forming an estimate of any work is that of analysis. It is impossible to compare the qualities of a composition with the standard in our mind, without separating those qualities from each other. We must be able to say that this passage has Force, that that has Elegance; to see that the work as a whole possesses Force but lacks Clearness; and so on for any and all the characteristics which may be found. It is necessary to study the effect which a work produces, and again to be able to tell upon what means those effects depend. In no other way can we put ourselves in a position to estimate fairly and conclusively the value and the lasting merit of that which we criticise.

I have more than once reminded you that literary work that is worth the name is a severe labor. It has never seemed to me worth while to attempt to lure you on with delusive persuasions of easy roads to literary perfection. All literary work which is worth doing is laborious and long; and of all literature which is generally included under the head of belles-lettres it seems to me that criticism is intellectually the most severe. It is so largely a matter of pure intellect that it even seems more arduous than it is. In writing poetry or fiction, or indeed any purely creative work, the pleasure of creation arouses the emotions and kindles the fancy. One can now and then give the rein to his mind, so to say, and let the steeds of his imagination start off for a dash. In criticism the imagination has no office save that of being sympathetic and of entering into the mood of another. The strain on the attention and the judgment is constant; and that there are no more good critics is to be accounted for by the explanation— which is almost an excuse—that criticism is so difficult an art.

When all other qualifications for criticising have been considered, there remains that most elusive, most essential of all,—taste. Taste is a fine sense of the fitness of things; a perception of the proper proportion in work, and of the limits to which the expression of feeling or emotion can go. It is closely allied to a sense of humor in its quality. It is no less a delicate appreciation of the fitness of means to effect, and of the propriety of the ways by which an author has endeavored to impress his readers. Taste is the self-respect of the imagination. It determines the line beyond which the fancy cannot go with dignity.

It is that faculty by which we decide that one shade of incongruity is humorous and touching, yet that the shade but a trifle deeper is vulgar and repulsive. The knowledge how far things should be carried; sensitiveness to literary propriety; delicacy to finest differences of effect, are all dependent upon this faculty, which underlies all æsthetic perception. How to improve it, refine it, develop it, is the question of all culture. Goethe says:—

> Taste should be educated by contemplation, not of the tolerably good, but of the truly excellent.... The best ... when you have fully apprehended, ... you will have a standard, and will know how to value inferior performances without overrating them.—*Conversations.*

There is little that can be added to this. The best books well read will do all for the taste that definite outward cultivation can do. The rest is a matter of inner growth. No one is fitted to criticise work until he has learned to appreciate work. Even a felon may claim to be tried by his peers, and surely an author is fairly entitled to at least this grace. The peer of an author in this sense is the man who sympathetically is able to understand him; who is trained to perceive what is the aim of a book, and so is in a position to judge how far it has succeeded or failed. Until one is conscious of having attained to this he should at least be modest in his judgments; he should define his opinions for himself, but he will not claim that infallibility which belongs only to the critic of the highest rank and which is claimed only by those of the lowest.

All this has to do with criticism as it should be, and as it is at its best. This is what men like Sainte-Beuve, Leslie Stephen, Taine, Lowell, and those of their rank have made it. If the question is that of writing what are called criticisms for the press, and especially for the daily press, the matter is not entirely the same. A newspaper is a business enterprise. The publishers have not established it in the interest of abstract virtues, and they generally care neither more nor less for ideals, whether literary or otherwise, than the broker or the banker next door. They conduct their business very much as business which depends directly upon public support is conducted everywhere. They endeavor to learn what the largest number of buyers will like, and this they endeavor to supply. If too many newspapers of to-day are nothing more or less than mental dram-shops or bagnios, the men who have not too much principle or self-respect to keep them have at least the defense, such as it is, that they print what the public proves itself most eager to buy.

The general public is neither willing nor able to enjoy genuine criticism, and the publishers do not give it to them. Criticism as it is to-day practiced as a matter of literary work, is apt to mean the writing of perfunctory book-reviews, notices of plays and concerts and pictures, all to entertain the reader or to provoke him to buy. There are a great many persons, moreover, who either have no time to read, or no mind to read the books of the day, yet who wish to appear to have opinions in regard to them. It is for this class that the great bulk of book-reviews are written. The publisher of a newspaper is aware that by furnishing what will with the unthinking pass for opinions he can on the one hand please unintelligent subscribers and on the other gratify the book publishers from whom come advertisements. There are very many reviewers who are too honest to say a thing which they do not believe, yet who are aware that if they said all that they think they would not be able to hold their places for a day. I do not wish to be unjust to the newspapers. I am too lately out of an editorial chair myself to be in a position to reflect upon them too hardly. I must say, however, that it is the aim of every newspaper to please the publishers if it is possible, and that there are not half a dozen in the country—if there are any—which are not in their reviews influenced by other considerations besides the merit of the works noticed. I should as soon think of taking my political opinions from a paid stump-speaker as my literary judgments from the book-reviews in a newspaper. The intellectual furnishing of a mind which is guided by them is like the plenishings of a room supplied with second-hand furniture purchased on the installment plan and decorated with cigarette-advertising lithographs.

In its high and proper sense, however, criticism is not alone a matter of literature, but of life as well. Culture is mainly a matter of self-criticism. We do not really know unless we are fully aware what we know. In other words, the distinction between conscious knowledge and vague impression is the measure of development. The correctness of self-estimate marks the difference between the cultivated and the uncultivated mind. It might on first thought seem as if this confounded culture with self-consciousness. On the contrary it distinguishes it from that painful weakness. Self-consciousness arises from a doubt of the mind; an inability to tell what is one's true value and one's true place. Culture is a fair and reasonable appreciation at once of one's mental merits and shortcomings; a knowledge of one's intellectual rank. This fairness of estimate enables the possessor of this quality to take his intellectual place without false shame on the one hand or false pride on the other; two faults which are the warp and woof of self-consciousness. Education is not acquisition, but assimilation; and assimilation is impossible without that mental judgment which is the best and final form of criticism. Mental advancement is possible only by the establishment in the mind of well-defined standards, and the measuring by them of the thoughts, the ideas, the opinions; and to establish definite standards and to measure by them is criticism, the tonic of the mind.

XXII

Style

The question which these talks set out to consider was what one can do to learn to write well. I began by saying that there are two sorts of power which enter into literary production, the communicable and the incommunicable, that which may be taught and that which is inborn, the technical and the imaginative. Naturally we have discussed chiefly the power which may be learned, those details of structure and of quality which depend upon means which we are able to analyze. The subject of which I wish now to say a little is connected rather with those powers and qualities which can be directly neither acquired nor imparted. We cannot close without some consideration of Style, that thing most elusive and intangible in its elements, yet most definite and recognizable in its effects; and Style in its more exact sense is a matter which has to do less with the mechanics of literature than with the creative impulse of the mind. Regarded in its higher aspect it is closely linked with the imagination, that faculty which, if the figure were not too mathematical, one might call reason raised to the nth power.

The term style is commonly used rather indefinitely to indicate either technical finish or the more subtle qualities of literary expression. Of course as far as it is to be understood in the former sense, we have been discussing it from the very beginning of these talks. If we understand it to mean merely correctness or even elegance of language, the proper proportion of the different parts of a composition, the accurate choice of words and the judicious employment of figures and of ornaments, we may be said to have dealt with all this in the previous lectures.

If I were to attempt to sum up concisely the more important points of what I have said, hitherto, it would be possible to cover a large portion of the ground by saying that the secret of literary ease and finish lies in attention to details. In my youth and in the dame-school in which I began to learn to write it was the fashion to set down moral and improving sentiments in the copy-books, and one of them was the sententious maxim with which you are all familiar,—"Trifles make up perfection, but perfection is no trifle." The hackneyed saying is a good deal nearer to being exact than are most didactic aphorisms. It is certainly true that though perfection is above all trifles yet a trifle may spoil it. The slightest touch breaks a bubble, and a single bad epithet will spoil a passage otherwise effective. To neglect details is to neglect the whole.

It is true that to consider only details is to deprive the work of all unity. It is like finishing carefully all the pieces which are to be set in a mosaic and neglecting to consider the design of the whole. I need not repeat here what has been said of the need of dealing with any literary work as a unit; but it is necessary to keep this in mind. Conceive a thing as broadly as possible. Look at it in the large; see it as clearly as you are able in its general outlines; and make it the aim of your labor to embody in words this broad conception firmly and clearly. When this is accomplished go over your work with a microscope to discover if there be anything in it which will prevent or injure the effect. Indeed, if you hope to be finished artists in words, it will be necessary that you see to it that every detail not only does not lessen the effect of the whole, but that it is a positive advantage and addition. It is only by such care in the management of trifling particulars that the finest results are to be obtained.

Going beyond all these largely mechanical matters, we come to the consideration of a more intangible, and yet a higher thing.

Suppose that you came upon these three passages in some book which did not give their authorship. Could you, although you had never seen them before, suppose that they had been written by the same author?—

Of this thing, however, be certain: wouldst thou plant for Eternity, then plant into the deep infinite faculties of man, his Fantasy and Heart; wouldst thou plant for a Year and Day, then plant into his shallow superficial faculties, his Self-love and Arithmetical Understanding, what will grow there. A Hierarch, therefore, and Pontiff of the World-will we called him, the Poet and inspired Maker; who, Prometheus-like, can shape new Symbols, and bring new Fire from Heaven to fix it there.—*Sartor Resartus*, iii. 3.

The figure of that first ancestor, invested by family tradition with a dim and dusky grandeur, was present to my boyish imagination, as far back as I can remember. It still haunts me, and induces a sort of home-feeling with the past, which I scarcely claim in reference to the present phase of the town. I seem to have a stronger claim as a resident here on account of this grave, bearded, sable-cloaked and steeple-crowned progenitor,— who came so early, with his Bible and his sword, and trode the unworn street with such a stately port, and made so large a figure, as a man of war and peace,—a stronger claim than for myself, whose name is seldom heard and my face hardly known.—*The Custom House.*

An obese person, with his waistcoat in closer connection with his legs than is quite reconcilable with the established ideas of grace, with that cast of feature which is figuratively called a bottle-nose, and with a face covered all over with pimples. He had been a tender plant once upon a time, but, from constant blowing in the fat air of funerals, had run to seed.—*Martin Chuzzlewit.*

Whether the reader recognized in these passages the hand of Carlyle, of Hawthorne, and of Dickens would of course depend upon his experience; but if he had any susceptibility to literary expression, he would appreciate the fact that they are somehow different. He would feel the distinction which arises from those essential qualities, both of matter and of manner, which distinguish one piece of literature from every other composition whatever. To the sum of these qualities we give the name Style. Style in this sense is the individuality of a work. What personality is to a human being, that is style to a composition. Indeed, one would be doing no great violence to language who defined this quality as the "personal equation" of a work.

Style is the personal impress which a writer inevitably sets upon his production. It is that character in what is written which results from the fact that these thoughts and emotions have been those of the author rather than of any other human being. It is the expression of one man's individuality, as sure and as unique as the sound of his voice, the look from his eye, or the imprint of his thumb. It is the quality which gives to the work of a master-mind, a mind in which the intellectual individuality is well developed, a flavor so unique that no man familiar with literary effects can mistake it for that of any other. It is style in this sense which is proof of authorship so conclusive that if we had authenticated and solemnly sworn declarations from both Shakespeare and Bacon that the latter wrote the plays attributed to the former, we should still know beyond all peradventure that this could not be. The final appeal in a case of doubt of authorship is the internal evidence. I do not mean to assert that mistakes may not arise here as in all other human affairs; but I do mean that it is inconceivable that any great imaginative work should be produced which should fail of bearing in it the incontestable mark of its author's personality. We say that one writer imitates another's style so cleverly that it is not possible for the counterfeit to be distinguished from the real. This may sometimes be true of the trifles of literature, though I doubt if even here the genuine expert could not detect the imposition. In those writings in which a genius has expressed his inner being, in which his imagination has unveiled itself, in which that true self that dwells in every human creature and with which we sometimes feel that we are hardly acquainted in our own case,—in these it is impossible that the stamp of his personality should not be impressed upon the work. It follows in the case mentioned that one thing of which a literary man is pretty likely to be sure is that whoever wrote the plays attributed to William Shakespeare, it is outside the limits of conceivable literary or human possibilities that they were written by the author of the poems and essays avowedly the work of Francis Bacon. There are those who would deny the truth of this illustration, I believe, but there is nobody who denies that an imaginative writer stamps the character of his mind upon his productions.

This matter of individualism is one of the most elusive and yet one of the most tangibly persuasive of all matters connected with literary art. Suppose two authors to be equally correct, equally well informed, well trained, and to write upon subjects in which we are equally interested. It will still be true that one will please us more than the other. There will be a certain quality, an almost intangible flavor about one book which is lacking in the other. One author will maintain a dignity in his attitude toward his subject, or he will possess a persuasive manner; in one way or another his individuality will charm us. We say that we are pleased with his style. We mean that the individual quality of what he writes has attracted us. To go back a little farther in analysis, what we say means practically that in the nature of the mind and the character of the author there is that which appeals to us as human beings or to us in particular as individuals. Here we touch upon an important principle which underlies this whole matter. The secret of charm in style lies in character. You have all heard innumerable times the saying that "Style is the man." In other words, style as a matter of structure in composition is the indication of what a man can do; style as a matter of quality is an indication of what he is.

The ways in which individuality shows itself are numerous. Each writer, for instance, may be said to make his own vocabulary. He consciously increases his knowledge of words, deliberately chooses certain terms for particular uses, and carefully decides upon the especial term which in each case seems to him best adapted to convey his meaning. Besides this he unconsciously has a preference toward this word or that, he is influenced by association, by the suggestions which are aroused in his mind by this synonym or that, and is in every decision swayed in one direction or another by the fineness of his perceptions, the nature of his temperament, and by all those minute and mingled elements which make up what we know as character. All these conscious and all these unconscious causes help to bring it about that every writer shall make for himself what Walter Pater calls a "vocabulary faithful to the coloring of his own spirit;" and the same principle may easily be traced through all the divisions of the literary art, whether they be of structure or of quality.

It follows that to talk of style in the higher sense is to consider character in its broadest and deepest extent. It is impossible to discuss any question of human life to its farthest limits without finding that it rests upon an ethical basis. The best method of phrasing aspiration and passion in art cannot be determined until we have searched out the nature of passion and of aspiration; until we have fixed upon some theory of man's relation to life and truth, and this is what is meant by ethics. If one examined far enough, it is probable that it would appear that the same is true of things which seem to us infinitely trivial. There is as truly a moral reason why children making mud pies in the gutter should not quarrel as there is that Dante's "Divine Comedy" is an immortal work. If we search deep enough, the reason why the children are amused by their mud pies is as surely to be found in the relations of human beings to life as is the reason of the spiritual exaltation which may come from the appreciative reading of the poet. I said the other evening that it might seem that I had a tendency to speak of English Composition as if it involved the whole duty of man; we have now come to the place where it is evident that it does. We cannot go into so extensive an examination as the foundation of morals and the elements of character, so that I shall content myself with pointing this out, leaving each to make—or not to make, as he pleases—such reflections and such deductions as fit his own need and his own inclinations.

It is strictly in the line of literary work, however, to comment once more upon the use of books in intellectual development as applied to style. What a man reads affects what he writes indirectly by its effect upon what he is, as we have before seen that it has a direct and swift agency in shaping his methods of expression. What the company he keeps is to a man's character, this to his style are the books he reads. A writer cannot accustom himself to the pages of the masters of literature and be content to write meanly and incorrectly. He may not consciously contrast his work with theirs, but the influence of their example is with him always. In very trying circumstances, I once said to a workman against whom falsehood seemed to be proved, "In spite of everything, I do believe that you have been telling me the truth." He answered me with a simplicity which was nothing less than noble, "If you knew my wife, sir, you'd know that I couldn't live with her and lie." I learned afterward that this was the exact state of the case. His wife was a rather silent woman, and I do not believe that she had ever lectured her husband on truth-telling. It was simply that one could not live in her influence and be willing to be guilty of falsehood. In the same way one cannot live familiarly with good literature and knowingly write bad.

It is not that one imitates good authors. Any imitation is bad art, because there should always be in what is done the ring of genuine, personal conviction. The imitator is not giving expression to that within him which is so real and so strong that it will not be suppressed. He is trying to show that he can feel as some one else has felt, that he can write as somebody else has written. It is a sham, and the reader feels that it is a sham. Imitation, moreover, is at best but a reproduction of the more obvious peculiarities of work, while at worst it is a catching of tricks, mannerisms, and faults. It may be added, too, that it is oftener at its worst than at its best. Anybody can imitate the defects of a style, and few its virtues.

In these days nobody reads avowedly for style directly. There was once an idea that it was well to select an author of standing and deliberately attempt to catch his manner, or, as the phrase went, to "form one's style on the master." The idea was about as sensible as would be the notion that it were well for a young man not wholly satisfied with his features to "form" his nose after that of the Apollo Belvedere. Style is the expression of selfhood. No writer can embody his own individuality in the expression of the individuality of another. Learn from the masterpieces what is good use in diction, in construction, in arrangement; learn from them to be strenuous, persuasive, and sincere in whatever you do; but do not for a moment think of obtaining from them that personal flavor which can come only from the writer himself, and which is the thing which makes style in its highest sense.

It is the development of the personality of the writer which saves a composition from becoming mechanical. In the first of these talks I quoted the instructions which Flaubert gave to Guy de Maupassant, in which he said:—

> Whatever may be the thing which one wishes to say, there is but one word for expressing it; only one verb to animate it, only one adjective to qualify it. It is essential to search for this word, for this verb, for this adjective, until they are discovered, and to be satisfied with nothing else.

This I commended to you as sound and necessary advice. From our present point of view, however, it is to be seen that this is the attitude of a student rather than that of an artist. In other words it is rather the way to learn to write than the way to write. So painfully minute a method as that which Flaubert recommended to his pupil would bring to an end all spontaneous or impassioned writing. The mind should be trained by these severe and careful methods until exactness of expression becomes a second nature. Then for good or for bad one must write as one is impelled to write at the particular moment. In revision the most strict requirements may be held to, so long as there is kept in mind the danger of revising the life out of imaginative writing and of refining until spontaneity is lost. Work should be revised with patient, with inexhaustible care; but it must be revised delicately. No formal correctness, no perfection of epithet or propriety of diction, can atone for the sacrifice of the intangible qualities which in the original form express the mood of the writer, and are to a composition what the personality is to a human being.

In all the talks which preceded this we have been considering work as that of the student who is preparing to write rather than as that of the author who is actually producing. When we talk of style we are dealing with the production of literature. The student who has not mastered details in the most painfully minute manner has not fitted himself for that perception of a subject on broad lines which is the condition of successful production. William Blake has said: "In order to know what is enough, it is necessary to know what is more than enough." The student must have acquired thoroughly the highest degree of elaboration possible in order that he may be able to judge what is proper and effective in any given case. He cannot fairly judge how far it is safe to go, unless he is keenly aware of what it is to go too far.

In considering a literary work as a whole and in treating it as an expression of his own particular and peculiar individuality, it is well for a writer to bear in mind a phrase of Mr. George Saintsbury, the English critic. "The first rule of literature," he says, "is that what is presented shall be presented not merely as it is, but transformed, and, if I may say so, *dis*realized." This is easily and obviously true of fiction. It is manifestly impossible to give a realized picture of life as it actually exists, to tell everything which must have happened to characters, how they eat and sleep, shiver when getting into their baths in the morning, find their egg too much or too little cooked at breakfast, get out of breath in hurrying to catch a street-car, and all the rest of the innumerable trifles which make up the bulk of life. On this plan the simplest story would be expanded into as many volumes as "Clarissa Harlowe." The same principle of selection and departure from reality is no less true of everything which is written. The thoughts which a philosopher weaves into a profound system do not come to him in sequence, beautifully arranged. If he followed the actual order of nature, he would put down a heterogeneous mass of reflections, good and bad mingled together, with no system apparent in them except after a painful study which no reader would be at all likely to give to the confused and confusing pages. Art is not nature. It is not the reproduction of nature. It is the invention of man to produce at will and to enshrine in permanent form those impressions, those emotions which come to him in rare and fleeting instants when his own consciousness reaches for a quick moment to the secret of that life which informs nature. Remember that the object of writing is not to reproduce the actual; that it is not even wholly that very different thing, to produce an impression of the actual; it is to embody and to make evident the truth which actualities express. Whoever takes up his pen to produce literature undertakes to make clearer the relation of man to nature and to life. He sets out to say in all sincerity what some fact of existence means to him. If he is content to be a mere scribe, simply an artisan of letters, he may deal with words in a mechanical fashion, and manufacture composition as one makes a deal table. This is honest work enough, but it is not the production of literature. It is the work of the hack-writer; of the reporter of life and not of the interpreter of life. To produce literature there must be an earnest attempt to embody the writer's conception of some phase of existence. There must be that expression of his convictions and character which is what we mean when we use the word style in its higher meaning.

It is of style in this sense that Goethe was thinking, when he said:—

It is not language in itself and independently which is accurate, vigorous, lucid, or graceful, but the spirit which is embodied in it; and so it is not in the power of every one to give to his work the good qualities of expression that should belong to it. The question is whether nature has given to the writer intellectual and moral qualities which demand and shape out for themselves such an embodiment as he has given them]—intellectual powers of intuition and penetration; and not less moral power, that he may be able to resist the evil demons who would hinder him in the unswerving loyalty that he must pay to truth.— Goethe: *Natur-Aphorismen*, iv.

There is no better way of testing what one has written than by comparing it with the work of great writers. See wherein their work excels yours. Do not thereupon say to yourself, "Oh, of course I am not to be expected to do as well as they." Say rather: "In so far as my work has fallen short of the best that has been done, it has fallen short of what has been shown to be possible. Let me see how far I can bring it nearer to the standard."

In the second of his "Discourses on Art," Sir Joshua Reynolds says to his students of painting:

Comparing your own efforts with those of some great master is indeed a severe and mortifying task, to which none will submit but such as have great views, with fortitude sufficient to forego the gratifications of present vanity for future honor. When the student has succeeded in some measure to his own satisfaction, and has felicitated himself on his success, to go voluntarily to a tribunal where he knows his vanity must be humbled, and all self-approbation must vanish, requires not only great resolution but great humility. To him, however, who has the ambition to be a real master, the solid satisfaction which proceeds from a consciousness of his advancement (of which seeing his own faults is the first step) will very abundantly compensate for present disappointment.

This need not be said differently to apply to the student of literature.

There is one thing of which he who desires to write literature may be sure, and that is that the unpardonable sin in this as in all art is flippancy. Flippancy is the prevailing literary vice of the age. The periodicals are perhaps more largely to blame for this than any other single cause, but newspapers and magazines by no means have the whole responsibility in this matter. The desire for amusement has eaten us up. The overworked and nerve-shaken public desires entertainment which shall make no call on the intellect and as little as possible on the perception. The man who could devise the means of amusing his fellows without their being obliged even to take the trouble to be aware of it would almost be deified by this age. The modern imagination is harder to awaken than the Sleeping Beauty. An audience at the theatre to-day cannot be persuaded to do anything for itself. In the days of Shakespeare a placard on the stage transferred all the beholders into the Forest of Arden or to the enchanted isle of Prospero. To-day it is difficult to induce the spectators to second the most elaborate devices which have been contrived by scene-painter and carpenter to assist their sluggish fancy. There is even a large class apparently so completely atrophied mentally as to be unable to follow a simple plot on the stage. "Variety shows" to-day take the place which real plays held once; short stories with only so much substance as admits of their being beaten up like the white of egg on a custard are languidly read by the million; and we have even replaced criticism by a sort of shallow flippancy for which no other name seems to me so appropriate as literary skirt-dancing. To be clever in the most superficial sense of that word, to be vulgarly glib, to reverence nothing, and above all to be smart and amusing, seems to be the sum and substance of the creed of writers who practice this art. They substitute adroitness for depth, scoffing for sentiment, and rapidity for brilliancy. Their one aim is to entertain the idle mind, and to win from astonishment the applause which they have not the wit to gain from approbation. The literary gymnastics of writers of these flippant pseudo-criticisms are hardly more intellectual than the supple evolutions of the ballet girl, and it is to be doubted if the dance is not the more moral and less debasing of the two.

This may sound extravagant, but when the influence upon young readers and young writers is considered it hardly seems possible to state the matter too strongly. It is true that these writers profess, so far as they profess anything, allegiance to all the highest virtues, both moral and intellectual. Their books are distinctly amusing—to those whose taste is not offended by the tone of flippancy which pervades them; and what they write is often eminently clever. Their fault is that they do not take life seriously; that they are as devoid of reverence as a stone is of blood; that their temper is as fatal to idealism, to enthusiasm, to aspiration, as carbonic acid gas is to animal life. Even the cynicism with which they are flavored is as sham as is the tint of a glass ruby. For a young writer to fall under this influence seems to me as great a literary misfortune as it would be a physical calamity for him to become crippled. If one wishes to earn a trumpery wage by writing smartly, these are his models; but if he is in love with literature, he must turn his back. The young writer should strive always to be serious before he is smart, sincere before he is clever, and to flee flippancy as he would flee the pestilence that stalketh at noonday.

By serious, I do not necessarily mean grave, and still less do I mean solemn. It is as true for the writer of humorous literature that he should take his art seriously as it is for the writer of history or of sermons. No man ever took literature more seriously than Charles

Lamb, yet he remains one of the most deliciously humorous writers of all time. He was gay and whimsical and droll, but he never for a moment failed of a high and noble respect for literature; he was apparently freakish, but he did not for a line become flippant. It would have been impossible for him to be vulgar. His taste always prevented his going too far. Even in the wildest excesses of humorous literature it is still absolutely needful to preserve a serious attitude toward literature and toward life. It is not that this feeling is to be obtruded. It is not meant that the jest shall be made with the sour visage of a Puritan. It is that the author himself shall never lose this inner respect and reverence for the dignities of life and for the truth. If these are a part of his character he cannot write otherwise than with them as it were forming a background to his work; and no literature is of lasting value or even fame which lacks this.

One of the most striking examples of what I mean is furnished by the poet François Villon, thief, house-breaker, and scape-gallows. He believed not in man, woman, or God, but he did hold to faith in literary art. Life as a matter of every-day existence he took flippantly enough, but literature as an expression of life he still regarded seriously,—and thus it happens that his poems live to-day, and that they are part of permanent literature.

Life is after all a serious matter to the lightest human being. However it is embroidered over with joys and jocund devices, with merriment or frivolity, every man knows its solemnity. There are for the most careless of men moments in which the real gravity of his situation, as he stands insecurely for a moment between the cradle and the grave, forces itself upon him. The only universal human experience is pain. To most men comes hope, and to most comes love in some degree of intensity. Joy, ambition, hate, and jealousy, are common to perhaps the great majority of mankind, and the writer who touches strongly and skillfully upon any one of these is sure of appealing to most readers. Only he who portrays sorrow and suffering is dealing with an experience so universal that he is sure that no man can fail of some appreciation of the theme. Such being the case, it is only the author who by his fundamental seriousness implies—remotely, it may be, but surely—that he has a share in the universal heritage, who can long or deeply command the attention of mankind. To be flippant is to be inhuman; and although the world may not analyze this, it is sure to feel it. Style is the unconscious revelation of the writer's attitude toward life, and if this be not serious all good gifts and graces of technical skill and mental cleverness, all adroitness of wit and strength of intellectual perception, even all vividness of imagination, will fail of making work great and permanently effective.

Volumes might be written upon style and its relations to authorship, but in the end it would still be necessary to acknowledge that the finest essence of literature is too subtle to be seized or analyzed. The aim of these talks was to consider the practical side of composition, and it is therefore aside from the purpose to attempt to discuss further the elusive æsthetic quality. Individual temperament and individual purpose must in the end determine what shall be the quality and style of all work; so that the secrets of this branch of literary art cannot be discovered until man is able to trace the nature and the working of those twin halves of the highest human consciousness, individuality and imagination.

Made in the USA
Monee, IL
07 July 2026